Measuring Business's Social Performance: The Corporate Social Audit

Measuring Business's Social Performance: The Corporate Social Audit

John J. Corson
and
George A. Steiner
in collaboration with
Robert C. Meehan

Committee for
Economic Development

Library of Congress Cataloging in Publication Data

Corson, John Jay, 1905–
    Measuring business's social performance.

(A Supplementary paper of the Committee for Economic Development, 39)
    Bibliography: p. 71
    1. Industry—Social aspects—United States.
I. Steiner, George Albert, 1912–   joint author.
II. Meehan, Robert C., joint author. III. Committee for Economic Development. IV. Title.
HD60.5.U5C69   301.5'5   74–19382
ISBN 0–87186–239–5

Printed in the United States of America

Committee for Economic Development
477 Madison Avenue, New York, N.Y. 10022

Contents

Foreword

When the late Raymon H. Mulford served as chairman of the subcommittee which prepared CED's policy statement on *Social Responsibilities of Business Corporations,* he convinced his fellow trustees that the statement should concentrate on the "large publicly owned, professionally managed corporations which account for most of the country's productive capacity and which generally bear the burden of leadership within the business community." The present study validates that judgment. The larger the size of the company, the greater its concern about social responsibility and the more likely it is to be working on a social audit or to expect that some form of social audit will be required in the future.

The larger companies of necessity must be more concerned about their integration with the rest of society, especially with those groups in society that constitute their most important constituencies. The view that business firms should concentrate only on their own profitability—behaving like mindless atoms reacting to the economic environment but unresponsive to the social environment—is, I hope, relegated to the archives, and to a few warlock economists who conjure up a world that never was. A few hundred large companies which account for the bulk of the nation's output largely determine the level of the economy and greatly influence the quality of our lives. Such companies cannot divorce themselves from their environment—be it physical, social, economic, or international. As the present volume demonstrates, the larger companies are quite aware of their importance and of ways in which they interact with the environment and their own constituencies. The study, therefore, again dispels the myth that the large company can for any extended period of time behave as though it were a small one whose actions are of little consequence except to its owners and employees.

There is a great gap, however, between the perception of the large company as a social organism and the way such an organism should effectively exercise its social responsibility.

This book modestly suggests in its last chapter the steps that each company might wisely take toward a social report fashioned to the company's own needs. The desirability of following this procedure in contrast with one calling for a uniform report for all companies is apparent and was clearly revealed in the responses to the survey. Some service companies—e.g., some consultants—saw themselves as being little concerned, as businesses, with pollution, urban renewal, or conservation. Others, like utilities, expressed major concern about these same areas. Social reports by the two types of firms would understandably be quite different in content and emphasis, but would overlap in such areas as education, the arts, and fair employment.

There is another consideration which also argues for reports tailored to individual company perceptions and problems. Philip M. Klutznick, chairman of the CED Research and Policy Committee, in a comment on this study, observed that it did not seem sufficiently to clarify the fact that "social targets are really moving targets, changing quickly in both priority and substance." The type of report that is suggested permits a company to take account of this—to eliminate the resolved problems of an earlier day and to add those unresolved problems that are emerging.

We can hope that a multitude of efforts over the years to make social reports would lead to the development of something like the common law in which consistency of cases would establish norms that might for some types of social performance be followed by most of the larger companies, and that common norms for other types of performance might be developed on an industry-by-industry basis by companies facing similar problems.

This study, whose authors have long been associated with CED as advisors, continues a series that stemmed from CED's dual interest in better educating business managers and in bringing about a better public understanding of business. Concern for achieving a better understanding of the social responsibilities of management led CED to build its twenty-fifth anniversary observance in 1967 around this theme, which culminated in the publication of *Business and Social Progress,* edited by Clarence C. Walton. The preparation of the policy statement *Social Responsibilities of Business Corporations* (1971) generated some path-breaking papers published as *A New Rationale for Corporate Social Policy* (1970). The present volume further extends a sporadic but continuing program of studies in this field.

We hope that those interested in this broader field of management responsibility will find this study to be a useful addition to the growing body of knowledge about corporate social responsibility and an inspiration for further progress. We are indebted to the companies responding to the questionnaire for their cooperation and to the authors for so skillfully weaving the responses into the main strands of thought about social responsibility and its measurement.

Alfred C. Neal
President
Committee for Economic Development

Measuring Business's Social Performance: The Corporate Social Audit

1

Social Responsibility:
A New Dimension of Corporate Accountability

Today, more than ever before, the American public is
interested in how large corporations conduct themselves.
(E. I. Du Pont de Nemours Company)[1]

American business enterprises—from the self-employed
appliance repairman to the billion-dollar corporation—are
being held responsible for their performance in a more precise
and thorough fashion than has ever occurred. The quality and
reliability of the services and products offered for sale must
meet steadily rising standards. The truthfulness and com-
pleteness of the information given consumers about the
services or products through labeling of advertising is subject
to continually exacting standards. The degree to which investors must be informed as to the details of a corporation's
financial operations, even its projections of revenues and
earnings, is greater today than at any previous time. From
August 1971 to May 1974 prices charged for many services
and products were subject to formal control by the federal
government. Even before this, however, the prices of some
services (e.g., medical care) and of some products (e.g., automobiles and steel) were increasingly subject to informal control in the court of public opinion.

Of more recent origin but part and parcel of this extended
demand for accountability is a growing insistence that corporations, particularly the larger ones, shall measure up to a

proliferating variety of social responsibilities. There is substantial evidence that "the public wants business to contribute a good deal more to achieving the goals of a good society"[2] and that individuals and groups (e.g., minorities, consumers, investors) alike want evidence with which to measure the contribution of business—positive or negative—to the well-being of society.

There agreement ends. There is no consensus on what is meant by the social actions of business, what social responsibilities it shall be expected to bear, how its performance in discharging them is to be appraised or audited, by whom the appraisal or social audit will be made, or to whom the findings shall be reported.

What is clear is that it is generally recognized that many of the actions of business firms (e.g., how many and who are employed, how scarce raw materials are utilized, the reliability and the safety of the products sold) affect the well-being of the society, and thus can be described as social actions. It is also clear that "business is being asked to assume broader responsibilities to society than ever before and to serve a wider range of human values"[3] (e.g., to employ the physically handicapped; to provide advancement opportunities for minorities; to assist in overcoming urban blight; to support educational, health, art, and other cultural institutions); these and similar expectations have come to be called social responsibilities. And the evolving means by which the corporation and others have striven to appraise the impact of its actions on the society and the manner in which it has discharged its social responsibilities have generally been described as a social audit.

The nature of these concepts and the evolution of the corporation's accountability for the discharge of social responsibilities is the subject of this book. Specifically, the variety of pressures for greater accountability and their sources are examined in this first chapter. The ways in which corporations are responding to these pressures are shown by a recently completed survey of 284 companies; that survey was undertaken to reveal what responsibilities corporations have assumed and how and to what extent they are taking stock of these activities. The third chapter assesses the logic and feasibility of meeting the growing demand for accountability through a social audit. The final chapter presents a series of steps that a firm may consider taking into account in assessing its social performance.

Guardians of the Public Interest

Among those who advance the notion of corporate accountability are the self-appointed guardians of the public interest. Several are prominent leaders in this community. Ralph Nader, the crusading lawyer and consumer advocate; Robert A. Dahl, professor of political science, Yale University; and Neil H. Jacoby, professor of business economics and policy, University of California, Los Angeles, articulate the underlying logic on which the views of this group are based.

Nader contends that what is needed is "a great national debate on the whole question of corporate accountability." The reason for this, he argues, is that:

> We're heading into a greater and greater portion of the economy taking on the characterization of corporate socialism, which is basically corporate power utilizing government power to protect it from competition, for example, oil import quotas; to grant large subsidies, for example, to the maritime industry; or to socialize the risk and costs of a lot of corporate activities through the tax mechanism or through inflated and constantly renegotiated contracts, for example, Lockheed.[4]

To assure that the concentrated corporate power he envisions is used in the public interest, Nader argues that the disclosure requirements of the Securities and Exchange Commission should be broadened to cover the whole impact of the corporation on society. He asks rhetorically: "Why shouldn't we know in the annual report how much U.S. Steel dumps into the water, air, and land—and where—as part of its social cost accounting?" Nader would supplement such disclosure with the requirement that each corporation maintain a complaint procedure and that each complaint be "fed into a national computerized system where it would be instantaneously available to the citizen."[5]

Professor Dahl has advanced views that imply the need for an assessment of the corporation's performance on an even broader front. Every large corporation, he contends, should be thought of as a social enterprise and as a political system that exercises "great power, influence, and control over other human beings." Dahl further states that "since 'external controls' on the behavior of large firms through markets and competition . . . are virtually worthless," and since neither stockholders nor management can be relied upon to ensure socially responsible behavior, other controls must be established.[6]

In proposing a remedy, Dahl goes far beyond Nader's basic requirement of disclosure. He recommends that a major investigation be launched by Congress to determine "the most appropriate ways to govern the large United States corporation in the foreseeable future." That is, Dahl asks, should the corporation be governed from without by the market, by the market supplemented by government controls, or from within by stockholders, by workers, by consumers, or by some combination of these groups? "What is the most appropriate form of ownership to achieve and maintain the kind of corporate government desired?" Congress should attempt to determine this as well as "the comparative efficiencies of different alternatives" of government and ownership; for example, can an enterprise be operated more efficiently under managerial control than under cooperative control? Finally, Congress should ascertain the advantages and disadvantages of scale. That is, "are large firms necessary in order to benefit from the advantages of scale?"[7]

The thrust of these questions is that such an investigation might demonstrate the need for the exercise of some greater control over corporate managements by government, stockholders, consumers, and employees. An even more likely result is that such an investigation would emphasize the necessity of providing each of these groups with fuller information about corporate affairs.

A rationale, which leads to less radical conclusions, for how the corporation may be made to serve the public interest, has been formulated by Neil H. Jacoby. He believes that the conventional theories of the past, which held that corporate behavior was dictated by "short-run profit maximization" or by the "security and business volume," are no longer tenable. It is now essential to recognize that "corporate behavior is responsive to political forces, public opinion, and governmental pressure." These forces, which are "all non-market forces," have "induced large companies to allocate resources to a variety of social purposes." Reciprocally, it follows that "political forces, public opinion, and governmental agencies are guided in their exercise of substantial power by such information and its accuracy as is made available (or is not made available) by the corporation itself."[8]

The observations and demands of these observers of contemporary corporate performance are certainly subject to debate. Their views are not presented here because they have general acceptance. Nor are their views set forth because they specifically call for a corporate social audit. They do not. Rather, these views are noted here because they demonstrate a growing demand for fuller information so that firms can be held accountable for the roles that different groups contend they should perform. We believe such demands will expand rather than diminish. The following discussion adds support to this contention.

Advocates for the Consumer

Closely affiliated with those concerned with guarding the public interest are the official and unofficial representatives of perhaps the most vocal group that now insists upon an evaluation of the social performance of business enterprises, namely, the consumers. The increased recognition of the rights and the strength of the consumer in the American economy is reflected in: (1) the accumulation of consumer protection legislation, for example, Flammable Fabrics Act

(1953), Fair Packaging and Labeling Act (1966), Truth-in-Lending Act (1968), and Consumer Product Safety Act (1972); (2) the existence of governmental machinery, for example, the special assistant to the President for consumer affairs and similar units in at least twenty-nine states and nine major cities or counties; (3) the new federal Consumer Product Safety Commission; and (4) a continuing volume of literature presenting the plight of the consumer or urging consumers to exercise their presumed economic power.[9]

The consumer is said to have four rights: to safety, to choose, to be heard, and to be informed. Implicit in the first three rights is the fourth. The presumption that the consumer will, if informed, act to protect his own safety, make wise and economic decisions, and voice his own views to producers is often challenged by evidence that consumers may still buy a shoddy product or service because it is the least expensive and remain silent about the lack of quality. Still, it is clear that if the consumer is to protect himself, let alone rule in the marketplace, he needs to be informed. Hence, each statute cited in the preceding paragraph specifically provides for the disclosure of information, and each governmental agency established to protect the consumer devotes much of its effort to forcing the disclosure of fuller and more reliable information. Much consumer-focused literature emphasizes that in a complex technological society advertising messages do not enable the average buyer to make intelligent choices between, for example, clothing made of Dacron or Fortrel, or competing automobiles, refrigerators, tires, or television sets.[10]

Investor's Need to Know

Corporate investors (a group that includes mutual funds, insurance companies, trust companies, trust departments of banks, pension funds, university or foundation endowments, and individuals) and their advisors are being confronted with both moral and economic pressures by some whose funds they handle and by social critics. Those who make investment decisions are increasingly being pressed to form moral judgments on the behavior of the corporations in which they might invest. They are now required to give recognition to the prospective impact on future costs and earnings of "unfunded past and future social costs" that society has imposed or is expected to impose on the corporations in which they would invest.[11]

The moral pressures bear with special force on those responsible for investing the funds of churches, universities, foundations, and other nonprofit institutions with similar social orientations. Together, these investors manage funds worth many billions of dollars. The executives responsible for these funds take various stands on the degree of pressure they should place upon corporations in which they are stockholders "to meet human needs and to ameliorate many kinds of current social problems, such as pollution, discrimination, unsafe conditions, and urban blight."[12] Some church, university, and foundation investors have stated that they do not condone particular activities engaged in by companies whose stock they hold, notably corporate operations in South Africa and the production of weapons with which the war in Vietnam was prosecuted.* Moreover, they have said that they will use their shares of stock to put ownership pressure on executives to engage in what they believe to be more socially responsive behavior.[13]

These investors seek information not generally made available upon which to base judgments about corporate behavior. The creation in December 1972 of the Investor Responsibility Research Center signaled an organized effort on the part of a number of large universities, foundations, and other endowed institutions to establish a basis for a more informed appraisal of the social behavior of corporations in which they and others have invested or contemplate investing. The essential function of the center is to offer those who sub-

---

*An example was provided by the World Council of Churches when it announced on January 22, 1973, that it had liquidated investments valued at about $1.5 million in British, Swiss, and Dutch companies doing business with white-ruled African countries. These investments represented 30 to 40 percent of the council's total shareholdings.

scribe to its research and information services an audit of the social behavior of corporations.

Economic pressures confronting investors are recognized by a small but increasing number of their spokesmen. The guidelines set by the American Bankers Association for use by the trust officers of banks reflect this awareness. These guidelines advise:

> A bank fiduciary should make every effort to make relative judgments on social and environmental issues [but] it would be improper . . . unless directed by its customer, to invest in the securities of a corporation solely because it has a good performance record in dealing with social and environmental problems, if investments in other securities . . . will produce a better financial reward.[14]

The Dreyfus Third Century Fund, one of the few mutual funds that focuses attention on corporations that avow an acceptance of social responsibilities, specifies what it takes into account in evaluations of the companies in which it invests. Its prospectus of March 1972 stated:

> The Fund will invest in companies which not only meet traditional investment standards but also show evidence in the conduct of their business relative to other companies in the same industry or industries of contributing to the enhancement of the quality of life in America. . . . The Fund intends to consider performance by companies in the areas of (1) the protection and improvement of the environment and the proper use of our natural resources, (2) occupational health and safety, (3) consumer protection and product purity, and (4) equal employment opportunity [and] special consideration will be given to those companies which have, or are developing, technology products or services which . . . will contribute to the enhancement of the quality of life.

The rationale for considering these factors is founded in the belief by managers of the Fund that performance at high standards in these areas "will generally indicate that these companies are well managed and, therefore, present opportunities for capital growth."

Three other mutual funds (First Spectrum Fund, Pax

World Fund, and Social Dimensions Fund) have announced substantially similar policies. If these funds persist in their efforts, they will tend to promote more socially responsive corporate behavior. Yet the managers of these funds have not made clear what guides they use in answering such basic questions as: What is socially responsive behavior? What standards exist against which the behavior of corporations can be measured? Is adequate information about corporate practice available?

To aid institutional and individual investors in formulating judgments regarding corporate social performance, the Council on Economic Priorities was established in 1970 by Alice Tepper Marlin to make in-depth studies of the policies and practices of particular companies and industries. The council serves both the investors who seek to weigh corporate social performance in considering investments and consumers who want to weigh such performance in choosing which products or services to purchase. The council's focus is indicated by the studies it has issued to date. One early report, *Paper Profits*,[15] assessed the extent to which each of twenty-four pulp and paper producers have installed antipollution devices and processes. A second report described activities of companies in the petroleum industry, and a third examined the environmental pollution practices of electric utility companies. Two further reports told subscribers of the involvement of a number of major corporations in the production of war matériel.

Reporting to Government

Governments, especially the federal government, are now requiring an accounting from corporations about their performance in a number of social program areas. However, reporting is piecemeal in the sense that each of a number of governmental agencies requires separate pieces of information about individual products, operational practices, employment practices, and financial operations. The consumer or the investor who desires to form an overall judgment of the social performance of a particular company can expect little help in integrating the various reports so that he can form that judgment, even if he could get the information.

Both the Food and Drug Administration and the Federal Trade Commission have required producers of products over which they have authority either to report the characteristics of products (e.g., through tests showing the safety or purity of drugs or the flammability of textiles) or to disclose specified information to the consumer (e.g., by labeling drugs, giving warnings on cigarette packages, and providing data concerning interest charges in consumer loan agreements). The information about product safety reported to these agencies has been supplemented since 1972 by the National Electronic Injury Surveillance System established by the Bureau of Product Safety in the Food and Drug Administration. This system, known as NEISS, provides periodic reports on the number of injuries to individuals in which a product was the cause.

The Environmental Protection Agency has set air pollution standards and has stimulated the state governments to establish water-quality standards. Corporations whose operations are covered must report periodically on their conformance with these standards.

The Equal Employment Opportunity Commission investigates the employment practices of corporations and requires the submission of data on employment of minority group members. The Department of Labor requires every establishment covered by the Occupational Safety and Health Act of 1970 to maintain a log of each occupational injury or illness suffered by an employee. This log must be available when the department's inspectors visit the establishment.

In June 1971 the Securities and Exchange Commission instituted new disclosure rules that require corporations to set forth in their financial statements the accounting principles that were used and the effect these principles had on the financial results reported.[16] Other new rules broadened the conventional areas of disclosure by adding requirements that each corporation disclose any prospective impact on capital outlays or earnings as a result of compliance with environmental control or civil rights legislation.[17] The commission is now being prodded by public-interest groups to force companies to include public-interest proposals suggested by shareholders in their proxy statements (e.g., the creation of a committee of General Motors Corporation shareholders to review the public impact of the company's management decisions).

Finally, the contracts signed by companies that do business with the federal government require them to perform various socially responsible actions and, in several instances, to report on their performance.[18] Firms that sell products or services to the federal government are required to maintain "fair employment practices," to provide "safe and healthful" working conditions, to pay "prevailing wages," to curb the pollution of the air and water, and to facilitate the employment and training of handicapped persons and of former prisoners seeking rehabilitation.

Role of the Accountant

As the growth of corporate enterprise has increased the impact of major corporations on investors, employees, consumers, other business firms, and the public, accountants have been pressed to accept steadily broadening responsibility for informing the society generally as well as their clients. They have, thus, "been caught in the bind between their public responsibilities and the pressure of clients who pay their fees."[19] Their response to this pressure has been manifested in the issuances of the former Accounting Principles Board, the establishment of the new Financial Accounting Standards Board, and the promulgation of guidelines by the American Institute of Certified Public Accountants. Their issuances have been reaffirmed by SEC rulings, and the courts have vigorously sought ways of providing all who read corporate annual reports with a fuller knowledge of the workings and projects of audited companies. One manifestation of this effort has been the development of what some now call socioeconomic accounting, a concept that embraces the assessment of corporate social performance.[20]

Accountants, like other observers of the current scene, have witnessed society's heightened concern with the quality of life. First, in noticing the vast sums being spent by governments for social programs, some accountants have come to believe that waste could be reduced by the application of their skills to the management of these programs.[21] Second, accountants have noted the emergence of the idea of indicators of social change, that is, measures of gain or loss in such areas as crime, education, health, and poverty reduction. Again, as professionals skilled in quantification and evaluation, they have visualized a role that they might play in refining the idea of indicators.[22] Third, and most relevant to this discussion, some have been considering how they can help a business firm to equip itself to cope with increasing demands for information about its social performance.

Each of the three professional associations of accountants has now established a committee to consider how they should go about measuring corporate social performance.† The work of the Committee on Social Measurement established by the American Institute of Certified Public Accountants is illustrative of these efforts. The chairman of this committee explains that "when business is being accused of an overpreoccupation with economic results at the expense of society at large, more and better information about social performance is clearly desirable." Hence, this committee is considering how accountants can:

1. Aid business to make plans and to formulate decisions that do a better job of taking external social impacts into account
2. Help business to make its own *pro bono publico* expenditures more productive
3. Report to the business's various publics, including the

---

†The American Institute of Certified Public Accountants, the American Accounting Association, and the National Association of Accountants.

government and regulatory agencies, on its performance as a corporate citizen

4. Enable investors, if and when they desire, to take social responsibility into account in selecting where to place their funds[23]

Even before this committee and the analogous committees of other professional associations report on their deliberations, some individual accountants experimented with the preparation of social audits for operating companies. One such experiment called a *social responsibility annual report (SRAR)* includes a summary statement describing the company and its operations. Also presented are factual data concerning "the social impact in the community," "the pollution of air and water," "occupational health and safety," "minorities recruitment and promotion," and "funds flow for socially relevant activities."[24] Another is described as a *socioeconomic operating statement (SEOS)*. It is "a tabulation of those expenditures made voluntarily to improve the welfare of employees and the public, product safety, or environmental conditions." Set against these pluses are certain "detriments," that is, the estimated costs of actions the company did not take and that, as a consequence, employees of the community had to bear; for example, the cost of safety devices or of pollution purification equipment the company did *not* install. Additionally the author of this proposal suggests that those businesses publishing a SEOS be allowed an extra tax deduction or credit for the net investment in social activities during the year.[25]

These prototypes are the initial attempts by accountants to apply their skills and experience in measuring corporate financial performance to the appraisal of a company's social performance. However, these prototypes may also be limited in their effectiveness because accountants' addiction to quantification and their limited familiarity with emerging social standards may handicap them in developing fruitful approaches to meeting the demands for information that reformers, consumers, investors, government, and responsible corporate executives will require in order to assess and compare social performance.

Executive Leadership

Business executives have led the way in the recognition of
the social responsibilities of corporations. Despite their close-
ness to the daily problems of operating their various enterprises profitably, which might be expected to influence their
judgments, they have come to see that corporations must meet
the noneconomic expectations of society. Indeed, read in the
light of questions being debated in the early 1970s, the words
and actions of Owen D. Young of the General Electric Company in the 1920s, of George Eastman and Marion B. Folsom
of the Eastman Kodak Company in the 1930s, of Paul G.
Hoffman of the Studebaker Corporation in the late 1940s, of
Frank W. Abrams of Standard Oil Company (New Jersey)
[now the Exxon Corporation] in the 1950s, and of J. Irwin
Miller of the Cummins Engine Company, and Arjay Miller,
then president of the Ford Motor Company in the 1960s, were
prescient.

The views of these early executives were updated in June
1971 by their modern-day counterparts in a statement on
national policy by the Committee for Economic Development,
Social Responsibilities of Business Corporations, which stated:

> Today it is clear that the terms of the contract between soci-
> ety and business are, in fact, changing in substantial and im-
> portant ways. Business is being asked to assume broader re-
> sponsibilities to society than ever before and to serve a wider
> range of human values .... Inasmuch as business exists to
> serve society, its future will depend on the quality of man-
> agement's response to the changing expectations of the
> public.[26]

> As the corporation adapts to the changing requirements of so-
> ciety, and moves into uncharted social terrain, there is a clear
> need to develop better methods for determining corporate
> goals and evaluating performance.[27]

Why do these business leaders propose that corporations
should accept these additional responsibilities, although they

would not result in any profits, and should accept the obligation of reporting to stockholders and to the public about their performance? A look back at the reasons voiced by those business leaders who (in their respective decades) assumed responsibilities for their companies that were not generally accepted and a look at recent happenings suggest three explanations for the course business leaders have taken.

The first explanation is that society's expectations of business have expanded over the years. Recent evidence of this is provided by a summary of public opinion polls conducted by Louis Harris over a six-year period. In February 1973 the Harris poll reported its findings as to what a sample of Americans stated as their expectations at three points in time (listed below). As can be seen in the list, nationwide cross-sections of the public have been asked this same question periodically since 1966, and there has been a steady rise in the proportion of respondents that expect business to take the lead in resolving the problems indicated.

The second explanation for the more socially responsive

"Do you think (READ LIST) is a problem that businessmen and companies should give some special leadership to, or not?"

	Should Give Leadership		
	1972	1971	1966
Controlling air and water pollution	92%	89%	69%
Eliminating economic depressions	88	83	76
Rebuilding our cities	85	84	74
Enabling people to use their creative talents fully	85	85	73
Eliminating racial discrimination	84	81	69
Wiping out poverty	83	81	69
Raising living standards around the world	80	74	43
Finding cures for disease	76	70	63
Giving a college education to all qualified	75	70	71
Controlling crime	73	64	42
Cutting down highway accidents	72	67	50
Raising moral standards	70	64	48
Reducing threat of war	68	61	55
Eliminating religious prejudice	63	52	37
Cutting out government red tape	57	50	34
Controlling top rapid population growth	44	43	17

behavior of business leaders is that many of them believe that if business does not itself resolve those social problems that it is equipped to cope with, government will enter the picture and assume the responsibility. A frequently cited example is the employment of ex-convicts, drug addicts, and persons similarly handicapped in finding jobs.

The third and most frequently cited reason businessmen give for their assumption of social responsibilities is that it is in their enlightened self-interest[†] to maintain a society in which private property is respected, private profits are permitted, and which is equitable, just, productive, rewarding, and secure. It is reasoned that the majority of the people are content to continue with laws and regulations that are hospitable to corporate operations when business leaders assume nonprofit responsibilities voluntarily.

Few would contend today that business has no responsibility for providing for those employees who after serving for many years are too old to work, for ensuring the safety and purity of the products it sells, for preventing the pollution of the environment, or for contributing to the maintenance of educational and social institutions. Even Milton Friedman, the most vocal opponent of business assumption of social responsibilities, has stated that business firms must "stay within the rules of the game."[28] Indeed, these social responsibilities have become accepted rules. Differences of opinion nevertheless do arise when it is proposed that businesses take on the additional responsibility of reporting to the public concerning its performance in the roles that it has assumed (at least in the first instance) voluntarily.

Viewed in the perspective of changes that have taken place in the last fifty years, it becomes clear that business has assumed large responsibilities for the welfare, safety, and

---

†*"Enlightened* self-interest is responsive to basic shifts in public attitudes (it is the wise bamboo which bends with the wind), consistently sensitive to human values, alert to subtle and indirect effects, and long in view. It is responsive to increasing expectations of openness and accountability." ("What Should a Corporation Do?" *Roper Report*, no. 2 [October 1971], p. 3. This appears in an excerpt of the philosophy and goals of the Standard Oil Company [N.J.], now the Exxon Corporation.)

equitable treatment of all employees; for safeguarding the interests of consumers; for protecting the environment; and for contributing to the well-being of society as a whole.

Everyone realizes, of course, that there are limits to the assumption of social responsibilities of business in general and for particular companies, whether they are government imposed or voluntarily undertaken. This is a very complex subject about which there is controversy, and this is not the place to examine it in any detail. Our views on this subject have been expressed elsewhere.[29]

Broadening Accountability

Accountability is not new for American corporations. In 1971 the Standard Oil Company (N.J.), now the Exxon Corporation, stated: "Historically we have had a responsibility to account financially to our shareholders. Now there is growing pressure for a broader accounting to a wider audience."[30] The demand for broader accounting has been described by one group of businessmen as "a fundamental shift from the principle that all business is essentially private and accountable only to stockholders and the free marketplace to legal doctrines that make large enterprises, in particular, more and more accountable to the general public."[31]

Pressures for accountability reflect the fundamental trend that Daniel Bell has termed "the subordination of the corporation."[32] He contends that, whereas the corporation was long judged in terms of individual contributions, it is being judged increasingly in terms of its contributions to, and the costs it imposes on, society as a whole. Individual satisfactions—those enjoyed by employees, consumers, and investors—can be assessed by the market. The satisfaction or dissatisfaction afforded society—stable, accident-free employment; safe, pure, and utilitarian products; and profitable, growing enterprises mindful of their impact on the physical and the social environment—cannot be evaluated in the marketplace.[33] Therefore, new means of appraisal are sought.

Concepts of the Social Audit

There are many different ideas about what a social audit is, and consensus on the subject is limited to the agreement that, at a high level of abstraction, the social audit is concerned with the social performance of a business in contrast to its economic performance as measured in the financial audit. Since all the definitions cannot be presented here, five basic types will be described.

First, some businessmen have concentrated on identifying and totaling expenditures for social activities. This concept, described as the "cost or outlay approach," involves the recognition of costs and the search for ways to reduce such costs. The application of this concept poses difficult problems of cost allocation. For example, what part of the cost of orienting and training a new employee should be attributed to the regular costs of doing business, and what part, such as the reduction of unemployment among black youths, should be attributed to the employer's undertaking of a social activity? The cost approach concentrates on inputs and makes no attempt to measure outputs—that is, how much social good and/or favorable public reaction toward the corporation have the dollars expended actually produced? It provides information needed to guide operating officials within the corporation but offers no measures of accomplishment that will satisfy the demands for information by consumers, the public at large, and government.

Second, the "human asset valuation approach to the social audit" is designed to measure the "value of the productive capability of the firm's human organization" and the "value of shareholder loyalty, banker and finance community goodwill, customer loyalty, supplier loyalty, and loyalty in the communities where plants or offices are located."[34] That these factors have values and that these values are influenced by the corporation's social behavior (e.g., the environment the firm provides for employees; the reputation for integrity it builds with customers, suppliers, and financiers; and the image it establishes in the minds of citizens) are ideas that are generally accepted. Hence, some students of the idea of a social audit propose the fulfillment of these values as a justification for the costs of social activities that the corporation carries on.

Those espousing this concept contend that it offers a "positive evaluation" of the worth of social activities and is preferable to a negative approach that focuses on costs and perhaps measures of what is done (e.g., number of women promoted above the supervisory level or the abandonment of billboard advertising). Critics of this concept, while accepting it as an aid to executive decision making and stockholder understanding, fault this approach on the grounds that it measures social accomplishments in terms that are not meaningful to constituents outside the corporation.

A third concept of the social audit has been described as the "program management" approach, which focuses on measuring only those activities in which a particular company is involved largely for social reasons. With respect to each such activity (e.g., the student loan program of a bank or the provision of scholarships for the children of employees of a corporation) this approach would involve (1) an approximation of the costs and (2) an evaluation of the effectiveness of the activity. The Bank of America has used this approach in assessing its activities, and its spokesmen argue for this concept in very pragmatic terms: Such "an audit appraises what can be appraised."[35] Thus, this kind of social audit serves the needs of corporate officials and provides some measures of accomplishment that meet the demands of certain external constituents.

A fourth concept, generally called the "inventory approach," involves the cataloging and narrative description of what the corporation is doing in each area where it recognizes that society (or articulate segments of society) expects it to do something. The results of this approach may be a massive descriptive listing of the corporation's activities with little or no analysis of results or costs. This approach does not provide a measure of the aggregate costs entailed; of the value to the company in terms of morale, goodwill, and public image; or of the benefits contributed to the society. It serves to inform the corporation's management and directors but provides less than is required to meet the demands of many outside the company who seek an evaluative accounting.

A fifth concept of the social audit can be called the cost/benefit approach. There are a number of possible types of cost/benefit analysis. One may be called the "balance sheet approach." This tries to quantify values contributed to society (assets) and detriments to society for actions taken or not taken (liabilities) and arrays them in a fashion comparable to the typical financial balance sheet.[36, 37] This is fundamentally an accounting approach to making a social audit and entails difficult and costly calculations. Very few companies have tried this approach. Another, simpler approach is to calculate costs of social programs and benefits, to the company and/or society, for programs undertaken, in either quantitative or qualitative terms. A number of companies have done this.

In actual practice, we have found no type of social audit that predominates either conceptually or operationally. There are combinations of approaches ranging from highly simplified descriptive statements to substantial documentation and quantification. The pressures for accountability suggest that a concept of the social audit that most businessmen may accept will likely evolve and that a standard operational format will be developed. That time, however, is far off.

Nonetheless, a surprising amount of interest and activity about the social audit is found in American business today, especially among the larger corporations. This is revealed in a survey of the business social audit completed in late 1973 by the authors, the results of which are presented in Chapter 2.

2

Survey of
the Social Audit:
Corporate Actions
and Opinions

Many of our political, economic, and commercial measures
of progress have become obsolescent. We need a new kind
of social accounting that goes beyond GNP for the nation
and beyond net profit for the firm. (Eli Goldston)[1]

Once corporations had gradually come to accept responsibility for a broad spectrum of social activities, some
business executives began to seek means to evaluate these
activities. During the late 1960s and early 1970s, an increasing
number of statements and reports describing or referring to
the initial efforts of corporations to evaluate their social performance became public. The very issuance of these statements and reports prompted the authors of this study to
undertake, with the encouragement and support of the Committee for Economic Development, the survey that is discussed
here. Our inquiry was designed to:

1. Reveal the extent to which American corporations are engaged in inventorying and appraising the social activities
   that they have undertaken
2. Indicate how the corporations had organized to carry out
   a periodic assessment of their efforts in these social
   activities
3. Describe the nature, number, and scope of the social activities that American corporations have undertaken
4. Identify the factors that survey respondents said had

prompted the decisions made to date to undertake activities
5. Indicate to whom (executives, directors, shareholders, the public) the results of these inventories and appraisals are being reported

Who Was Surveyed and How

The results of this survey show that a significant proportion of this country's larger corporations have made some effort to assess and report on the social activities they have undertaken. That conclusion is based on the replies obtained in response to a questionnaire requesting "views and facts about current business practices in assessing and reporting on performance concerning various social activities." The questionnaire was sent to 750 companies; usable replies were received from 284 companies. Most returned questionnaires were from larger companies, as is indicated in Table 1.

Eighteen industries were represented by those responding to the inquiry. Table 2 indicates that the bulk of the responses (48.3 percent) was received from companies in the manufacturing industries. Finance, insurance, and real estate companies contributed 27.9 percent of the replies; transportation, communications, and utilities contributed 12.1 percent. The remainder were in the extracting industries, wholesale and retail trade, and other services.

Table 1

Distribution of Respondents by Annual Sales Volume

Annual Sales Volume	Firms Responding	Percent Responding
Over $10 billion	22	8.6
Between $1 and $10 billion	96	37.4
Between $500 and $999 million	47	18.3
Between $100 and $499 million	79	30.7
Under $100 million	13	5.0
	257	100.0
Not reporting	27	
Total sample	284	

Table 2

Distribution of Respondents by Industry

Industry		Firms Responding	Percent Responding
Agriculture, forestry, and fisheries		1	.4
Mining		6	2.2
Contract construction		2	.7
Manufacturing			
Aerospace and transport equipment		15	5.5
Tobacco, food, and kindred products		23	8.5
Textile, apparel, lumber, furniture, and paper products		11	4.0
Chemicals		16	5.9
Petroleum refining		7	2.6
Rubber, plastic, and leather products		5	1.8
Construction materials		5	1.8
Primary metals		7	2.6
Fabricated metal products		10	3.7
Machinery		12	4.4
Scientific instruments and electronics		20	7.4
	Total	131	48.3
Transportation, communication, and utilities		33	12.1
Wholesale and retail trade		15	5.5
Finance, insurance, and real estate		76	27.9
Services		8	2.9
		272	100.0
	Not reporting	12	
	Total sample	284	

Acceptance of the Idea of the Social Audit

The concept that a corporation might or should subject its activities to a social audit is not a new one.[2] However, in actual practice, despite the pressures on corporations during recent years to assume responsibility for social activities, the social audit is still in its infancy. A few attempts to make social audits—by the Bank of America, Chase Manhattan Bank, Eastern Gas and Fuel Associates, Philip Morris, and Exxon Corporation—have come to public attention during 1968 to 1974, but little is known of the extent to which other corporations have taken stock of their performances in the area of social activities. Hence, the survey included this question: "Has your company attempted within the period since January 1, 1972, to inventory or to assess what has been done in any of a series of 'activity fields'?"

It should be noted that the term *social audit* was not used. However, a list of activities deemed to fall within the range of social activities was included in the questionnaire to ensure some common understanding of activity fields.

Seventy-six percent of all responding companies reported that they had attempted to make such an inventory or assessment. Of those companies that responded affirmatively, 89 percent had examined more than one activity field. The larger the company, the more likely it was to have undertaken such an inventory or assessment. Table 3 shows the number and proportion of all firms reporting, by volume of annual sales, that have made social audits, as interpreted by them.

The nature and extent of the effort that is here classified as the making of a social audit varies greatly among companies in the degree to which a mere inventory of what is being done is made and in the extent to which efforts are conducted to calculate the costs entailed and/or the benefits produced by social activities. The social audit varies in terms of the number of activities appraised and the amount of .executive manpower invested in inventorying and assessing. One indication of the fullness of the effort is provided by the answers to this question: "Has your company given any person, organizational unit or group responsibility for surveying more or

Table 3

Distribution of Companies Reporting That They Had Made a Social Audit

Annual Sales Volume	Firms Responding	Firms Assessing	Percent
Over $10 billion	22	22	100
Between $1 and $10 billion	94	78	82
Between $500 and $999 million	47	37	78
Between $100 and $499 million	79	50	63
Under $100 million	12	7	58
Total	254	194	76

less continuously the evolving demands on your company for
social action programs?" This question was answered affirmatively by 70 percent of the firms responding (Table 4). The
titles of the persons and staff groups to whom this responsibility has been assigned offers some basis for speculation about
the emphasis given to making and using the social audit. The
titles of these persons and groups are shown in Table 5. Analy-

Table 4

Distribution of Companies Assigning Responsibilities to
Group or Individual for Surveying Social Action Programs

Annual Sales Volume	Firms Responding	Firms Answering "Yes"	Percent
Over $10 billion	22	19	86
Between $1 and $10 billion	95	78	82
Between $500 and $999 million	47	32	68
Between $100 and $499 million	78	42	53
Under $100 million	12	7	58
Total	254	178	70

Table 5

Titles of Persons and Staff Groups to Whom Responsibility
for Social Programs Has Been Assigned

Title	Number	Percent
Public and community affairs department	71	42
Senior vice-president	23	14
Corporate relations	11	6
Environmental and urban affairs	19	11
Vice-president, personnel	11	6
Board of directors	5	3
Board committee on corporate responsibility	8	4
Senior vice-president, human resources	4	2
Corporate contributions committee	4	2
Employee relations	6	4
Assistant vice-president	3	2
Human resources management group	1	
Director of planning and budgeting	1	
Vice-chairman	1	3
Ad hoc executive task force	1	
Secretary of contributions committee	1	
	170	100

sis of the replies of those companies reporting the assignment of responsibility "for surveying more or less continuously the evolving demands on your company for social action programs" disclosed that the larger the company, the more likely it is to have established continuing arrangements.

Social Activities Undertaken

A list of the activity fields to be construed as falling within the realm of social responsibilities was included in the questionnaire. CED, in its 1971 policy statement on *Social Responsibilities of Business Corporations*, had described them as "the sorts of things being done by business in the aggregate." Fifty-eight activities covering ten fields of social responsibility were listed. Each respondent was asked: "Would you please check . . . which of the listed activities your company is engaged in? (In responding to this question please refer only to activities of your company within the United States. Also, please respond for the entire company. It is not requested that there be a response for each plant location.)"

This question was made more precise by the further definition of "engaged in," that is, to which of these activities had the companies made "significant commitments of money and/or personnel time?" Table 6 represents a summary of the answers to this question and indicates the ten activities engaged in by the greatest number of reporting companies.

Scanning Table 6 will show that it includes activities that corporations undertake voluntarily and others that they are compelled by law to carry on. It includes activities that are undertaken in order to make a profit and those that are performed without prospect of direct profit.

Moreover, as extensive as this list is, it does not encompass the range of activities for which the six constituencies identified in Chapter 1 would hold the corporation accountable. For example, the list presumes that the corporation is meeting the consumer's demand for the safety and reliability of the product; it does not ask whether the company is record-

Table 6. Number of Companies Reporting

Social and Economic Programs for Which They Have Made
Significant Commitments of Money and/or Personnel Time

Activity	Number of Companies Indicating Involvement	Ten Most Frequent Activities
ECONOMIC GROWTH AND EFFICIENCY		
Increasing productivity in the private sector of the economy	180	6
Improving the innovativeness and performance of business management	174	
Enhancing competition	69	
Cooperating with the government in developing more effective measures to control inflation and achieve high levels of employment	121	
Supporting fiscal and monetary policies for steady economic growth	109	
Helping with the post-Vietnam conversion of the economy	37	
EDUCATION		
Direct financial aid to schools, including scholarships, grants, and tuition refunds	238	2
Support for increases in school budgets	38	
Donation of equipment and skilled personnel	139	
Assistance in curriculum development	83	
Aid in counseling and remedial education	67	
Establishment of new schools, running schools and school systems	38	
Assistance in the management and financing of colleges	120	
EMPLOYMENT AND TRAINING		
Active recruitment of the disadvantaged	199	3
Special functional training, remedial education, and counseling	134	
Provision of day-care centers for children of working mothers	26	
Improvement of work/career opportunities	191	4
Retraining of workers affected by automation or other causes of joblessness	80	
Establishment of company programs to remove the hazards of old age and sickness	139	
Supporting where needed and appropriate the extension of government accident, unemployment, health, and retirement systems	93	
CIVIL RIGHTS AND EQUAL OPPORTUNITY		
Ensuring employment and advancement opportunities for minorities	244	1
Facilitating equality of results by continued training and other special programs	176	
Supporting and aiding the improvement of black educational facilities, and special pro-		

Table 6. Number of Companies Reporting *(Continued)*

Activity	Number of Companies Indicating Involvement	Ten Most Frequent Activities
grams for blacks and other minorities in integrated institutions	159	
Encouraging adoption of open-housing ordinances	31	
Building plants and sales offices in the ghettos	39	
Providing financing and managerial assistance to minority enterprises, and participating with minorities in joint ventures	134	
URBAN RENEWAL AND DEVELOPMENT		
Leadership and financial support for city and regional planning and development	135	
Building or improving low-income housing	75	
Building shopping centers, new communities, new cities	78	
Improving transportation systems	88	
POLLUTION ABATEMENT		
Installation of modern equipment	189	5
Engineering new facilities for minimum environmental effects	169	10
Research and technological development	145	
Cooperating with municipalities in joint treatment facilities	84	
Cooperating with local, state, regional, and federal agencies in developing improved systems of environmental management	126	
Developing more effective programs for recycling and reusing disposable materials	97	
CONSERVATION AND RECREATION		
Augmenting the supply of replenishable resources, such as trees, with more productive species	42	
Preserving animal life and the ecology of forests and comparable areas	41	
Providing recreational and aesthetic facilities for public use	80	
Restoring aesthetically depleted properties such as strip mines	38	
Improving the yield of scarce materials and recycling to conserve the supply	61	
CULTURE AND THE ARTS		
Direct financial support to art institutions and the performing arts	177	7
Development of indirect support as a business expense through gifts in kind, sponsoring artistic talent, and advertising	96	
Participation on boards to give advice on legal, labor, and financial management problems	138	
Helping secure government financial support for local or state arts councils and the National Endowment for the Arts	49	

Activity	Number of Companies Indicating Involvement	Ten Most Frequent Activities
MEDICAL CARE		
Helping plan community health activities	111	
Designing and operating low-cost medical-care programs	42	
Designing and running new hospitals, clinics, and extended-care facilities	42	
Improving the administration and effectiveness of medical care	89	
Developing better systems for medical education, nurses' training	52	
Developing and supporting a better national system of health care	40	
GOVERNMENT		
Helping improve management performance at all levels of government	100	
Supporting adequate compensation and development programs for government executives and employees	31	
Working for the modernization of the nation's governmental structure	51	
Facilitating the reorganization of government to improve its responsiveness and performance	69	
Advocating and supporting reforms in the election system and the legislative process	39	
Designing programs to enhance the effectiveness of the civil services	22	
Promoting reforms in the public welfare system, law enforcement, and other major governmental operations	62	

ing and reporting the number of product or service complaints received or potential liabilities ensuing from them. It presumes that the corporation is meeting the government's expanding demands for performance of a variety of activities; an audit of this list of activities would not reveal failures to conform with prohibitions against discrimination in employment or comply with standards for air and water pollution. Also, this list does not touch upon the concern some investors have expressed about corporations' operations in the white-ruled countries of Africa.

Some corporations indicated in their responses that they were carrying on activities not included in this list. The activities that one or more companies indicated they were engaged in, as stated substantially in their executives' own words, were:

Finding jobs and training opportunities with private employers for disadvantaged persons and Vietnam veterans in collaboration with the National Alliance of Businessmen (NAB)

Supporting basic and applied research to enhance the quality of life and to encourage economic growth

Carrying on drug-abuse educational programs for employees

Providing free drugs for indigent patients

Hiring Vietnam veterans

Hiring ex-convicts

Sponsoring sports events for local causes

On-loan personnel to business-government teamwork

Working to improve business management and education in local schools

Conducting regional planning studies

Participating in local fund-raising efforts to provide day-to-day care for persons qualifying under approved institutions, and spearheading fund-raising programs for new buildings, privately operated and managed, for organizations such as the YWCA, YMCA, Salvation Army, and others serving the indigent, the physically handicapped, and the mentally retarded

Participating in financial campaigns for new hospitals or extensions of existing hospital facilities

Providing management assistance to urban school systems

Considerable involvement in rehabilitation of physically handicapped

Sponsoring engineering education for minorities

Making capital grants for community hospitals

Minority purchasing efforts

Building a variety of retailing facilities within the inner cities

Purchasing from minority enterprises, and participating with minorities

Establishing a formal company employee policy on civic participation

Financing of public school facilities through the purchase of bonds

Training high school students and adults in sound personal money management

Matching-gifts program for employees

Financing low- and middle-income housing

Financing large volume of office, industrial, and high-rise residential property

Financing construction of inner-city hospital facilities; financing medical school education of future doctors

Participating through loaned executive in federal debt management

Maintaining plants and sales offices in the ghettos

Supporting tax legislation to improve local transportation

Contributing to charitable, educational, or civic activities by encouraging employees to serve as volunteers using company talent and expertise to develop public service announcements on both radio and TV, logotypes, brochures, advertisements, and billboard messages to support fund raising by charitable organizations

Supporting the development of black-managed banks

Explaining and promoting free enterprise

Improving management effectiveness in collective bargaining

Supporting public education by various promotional efforts and the provision of technical assistance

Promoting the development of housing, services, and activities for aged persons

Supporting industrial development of the areas in which plants and offices are located by the provision of funds and personnel

Assisting with various community development projects

Supporting proposed constructive legislation in areas of the company's activity, for example, environmental conservation

Improving appearance of low-income areas

Employing ex-offenders and ex-addicts

Supporting summer youth-work programs

Supporting ecological projects

Supporting national conference on mass transit

Providing opportunities for continuing education to employees

Obviously, this list of activities duplicates to some degree the activities included in the list provided in the survey. In some instances, the activities listed are of questionable value to the society, as distinguished from their value to the reporting corporations. They are, nevertheless, included here in order to illustrate both the broad range of activities in which the responding companies are engaged and the prevailing interpretation of social responsibility.

Why Make a Social Audit?

Each corporation was asked why it had undertaken to assess and in some instances to report on its performance of social activities, that is, to make a social audit. A list of possible purposes was provided, and respondents were asked to check those purposes that best explained their actions. They also were requested to write in additional reasons that may have prompted their actions. Some did so and also added meaningful statements describing their concepts of the social audit and their reasons for undertaking to make an audit. For example, one respondent stated:

> If the firm acknowledges that it has a responsibility to its community beyond that of profit-maker, it requires some means of evaluating its activities beyond its regular business operations. The social audit is the corporate tool which en-

ables the firm to take stock of its social posture with its extra-business activities. From this inventory, the firm can assess whether or not it is fulfilling the social responsibility which it defines for itself. Briefly, a social audit (a) reviews the firm's performance against accepted social objectives; (b) determines the dollar value of its commitment; (c) evaluates to the extent possible the social impact of investment decisions; (d) determines how much corporate social involvement is in the interest of the corporation.

Purposes of the Social Audit

A review of Table 7 shows that the principal reasons corporations have undertaken assessments of their social activities are "to examine what the company is actually doing" and "to appraise or evaluate performance in selected areas." The

Table 7

Purposes That Led Companies to Undertake Social Audits

	Number	Percent
1. To identify those social pressures which the company feels pressured to undertake	55	5
2. To identify those social programs which the company feels it ought to be pursuing	157	14
3. To examine what the company is actually doing in selected areas	194	17
4. To appraise or evaluate performance in selected areas	162	14
5. To determine areas where our company may be vulnerable to attack	101	9
6. To inject into the general thinking of managers a social point of view	122	11
7. To ensure that specific decision-making processes incorporate a social point of view	95	8
8. To inform the public of what the company is doing	70	6
9. To offset irresponsible audits made by outside self-appointed groups	41	4
10. To meet public demands for corporate accountability in the social area	78	7
11. To increase profits	37	3
12. Other	17	2

Note: A total of 196 companies checked one or more purposes.

demand for accountability from reformers, consumer advocates, investors, the government, and others is not high in the
list of the factors that prompted the undertaking of an audit of
social performance.

In order to present an accurate reflection of the motiva-
tions that have prompted corporations to undertake social
audits, Table 7 must be supplemented by the statements made
by a number of respondents on their questionnaires. Some
of the explanations of purposes were: "as a guide to internal
management," "part of marketing strategy," "part of long-
range planning," "to broaden experience and thinking of managers," "to extend markets with minorities and government,"
"to determine priority and urgency," "to balance commitment
to social activity against job activity," "to help those who need
jobs and housing," "to provide source material for executive
speeches and public statements," "to develop some reward-
accountability for managers," "to make sure the company is
fulfilling its promises and commitments," and "to provide
comprehensive response to many inquiries in this area." An
examination of these statements reveals that most corporations that have undertaken the inventorying and assessing of
their performance in the area of social activities have done so
for corporation-centered reasons. Only the last two statements
of purpose reflect an effort to meet the apparent external demand for them to account for their performance in this area.

Nature of the Social Audit

Many respondents linked the purpose of their examination of social activities with a definition of what such an
examination is or should be. Their statements on this point
contribute significantly to an understanding of the current
state of the social audit. For example, one respondent, after
suggesting that the term *social statement* or *social report*
would be preferable to social audit, added:

> A social statement, then, should be and, hopefully, will be-
> come an honest appraisal, sans puffery, of the actions taken

by an organization to alleviate social ills, whether such ills are among those which business is normally expected to correct (such as employment practices and pollution clean-up) or are far afield (such as drug abuse, nursery schools, and playgrounds). The statement should include specifics, i.e., that minority group employment has been increased x percent, that y number of females have been advanced to management positions, that z dollars have been contributed to black colleges. The debit side of the coin, suggested by some, should be omitted. What is to be gained by baring the corporate soul in acknowledging the dollars not yet spent (even though programmed) for a pollution-control device or the nursery one has not established for working mothers?

Another respondent defined the social audit as envisioned by his company as:

a summary of all the corporation's social impacts and interfaces expressed in quantifiable terms or at least in some form of balance sheet approach. The favorable factors might be listed on the "asset" side of the sheet and the unfavorable on the liability side of the sheet.

These statements emphasize quantification and the balance sheet approach in contrast to a purely descriptive social statement. They contrast also with the views volunteered by another respondent, who contended that "an audit must include":

1. An accurate status report of activity, location by location, based on clearly defined categories: hiring practices, promotional opportunities, training programs, minority purchasing, guaranteed loans to minority firms, specific community involvement, contributions and memberships, plant site selection, property disposal, and more
2. Written goals countersigned by upper management to improve performance, location by location
3. Continuous monitoring of action and a means to measure progress
4. Rewards for achieving goals; penalties for failure. Example: promotions, incentive pay, awards programs, etc.

Table 8

Obstacles Confronted by Those Corporations That Undertake Social Audits

Obstacle	Order of Importance*					Rank
	1	2	3	4	5	
1 Inability to develop consensus on ways to organize information	15	29	43	41	22	4
2. Inability to develop consensus as to what activities shall be covered	38	35	50	34	8	3
3. Danger to the company in publishing the results of social audits	8	18	15	14	66	5
4. Inability to develop measures of performance which everyone will accept	98	57	29	8	4	1
5. General decline in pressures on business to undertake social programs	9	7	5	7	73	6
6. Inability to make creditable cost/benefit analysis to guide company actions	58	63	25	32	8	2

*Companies identified 1, 2, 3, 4, 5 in order of importance.

Implicit in these varying opinions of the nature of a social audit are differing judgments concerning the feasibility of measuring accomplishments in various social activities. That effective measures are not yet available in many fields is indicated by the answers given to the following question: "What do you see as the most important obstacles to the development of social audits? (Please identify, if possible, 1, 2, 3, 4, 5 in order of importance.)" Table 8 presents the obstacles that were suggested and the relative importance attached to each by the respondents.

Future of the Social Audit

In considering the views expressed by corporations about the nature of a social audit, it is also necessary to take into account the future of such an instrument. Hence, the following question was asked: "In general, do you think that business firms will be required to make a social audit in the future?" Forty-six percent of all respondents (122) answered "Yes" to

Table 9

Respondents' Views as to Whether the Social Audit Will Be
Required in the Future

Annual Sales Volume	Firms Responding	Firms Answering "Yes"	Percent
Over $10 billion	22	13	59
Between $1 and $10 billion	90	37	41
Between $500 and $999 million	46	21	45
Between $100 and $499 million	75	34	45
Under $100 million	13	4	30
Total	246	109	44

this question. As is shown in Table 9, greater proportions of
the larger corporations foresee the probability that their firms
will be required to submit to a social audit.[3]

In order to delve more deeply into their views on the
future of the social audit, respondents were asked: "If your
answer is yes, please indicate whether in your opinion this
prospect is acceptable to you as a businessman." Some respondents simply said "Yes" or "agreeable"; others said "Yes"
and added some reservations; only four wrote in a flat "No."
Many respondents commented as to why they approved or
disapproved of the prospective requirement that corporations
submit to social audits. Their views afford valuable insights
into current managerial thinking with regard to corporate
social responsibilities; hence, they are presented in full in the
appendix.

Reporting Practices

Despite the growth, over a decade or more of public
opinion that corporations should do more for the social good,
the American corporation does not yet have an established
obligation to render an accounting to anyone on its overall
social performance. As noted in Chapter 1, it is required
to report, usually in quantitative terms, to a number of governmental agencies (including the Food and Drug Administration, the Environmental Protection Agency, the Department

Table 10

Recipients of Social Audit Reports

	Number	Percent
Executives only	79	38
Directors only	3	1
Executives and directors	29	14
Executives, directors, and stockholders	16	8
Executives, directors, stockholders, and the public	34	17
Executives, directors, stockholders, the public, and others	45	22
	206	100
Not reporting	78	
Total sample	284	

of Labor, the Securities and Exchange Commission, the Federal Trade Commission, and others) on particular activities. But the corporation has no obligation to provide the reformers, the consumers, the would-be investors, or the general public with a statement or evaluation of its social performance. Seen in this light, the answers of respondents (shown in Table 10) to the following question were predictable: "To whom were the results of this inventory and assessment made available?"

In response to a question about how the results of social audits were made public when such was the case, it was found that 45 percent of the respondents used the annual corporate report as the vehicle for public dissemination of information produced by the social audit. "All media" (e.g., reports, press, television, and radio) were used by 24 percent of the respondents; 17 percent made the results public by issuing a special report; 6 percent issued press releases to present the results; and 8 percent indicated that they used still other means.

Evolution of the Social Audit

Surveys of business practices such as the one reported on in this chapter are obviously not instruments for precise analysis, particularly when the practice, as this case, is a novel and evolving one. Opinions among those whose activities are being surveyed vary widely with regard to the logic and desirability of the practice. Furthermore, definitions of terms being used are not exact nor can they be made precise because of the evolving nature of the practice.

To stimulate thinking about evolving attitudes and practices among business executives and those who are demanding greater corporate accountability, we will in Chapter 3 consider:

1. An exposition of the logic underlying the social audit
2. A proposal concerning the scope (to borrow a term from the auditors) of the social audit
3. An analysis of the problems of measuring business's social performance

In Chapter 4, we will venture, in very tentative but still prescriptive terms, to suggest the course that corporations may well follow. As in other aspects of business practice, the old adage "nothing ventured, nothing gained" has a meaningful application.

3

The Logic, Scope, and Feasibility of the Corporate Social Audit

Some corporations are exploring the idea of making an annual audit of their operations—quantified to the maximum feasible degree—which would measure their responsiveness to social action. Because the concept is sound, the company social audit will probably come into wide usage. (Neil H. Jacoby)[1]

Is the social audit to become common corporate practice, or is it a fad to be abandoned in the years to come? To determine if the social audit is a valid concept requires consideration of three precedential questions.

1. Is the concept of the social audit founded on logical reasoning with regard to the relationship that does, or should, obtain between the corporation and the society?

It is most probable that less than one-fifth of all American corporations have as yet attempted to assess their social activities currently in terms of society's expectations. An indication that the very idea of responsibility to society for the performance of social activities is held by few corporate executives is suggested by the respondents' answers to two survey questions. When asked what purpose or purposes led management to undertake a social audit, a small minority attributed their action to the felt need for public disclosure or to their desire to "meet public demands for corporate accountability," (Table 7). When asked to whom the results of their audits were disclosed, the responses indicated that less than half these companies made their findings available to their stock-holders and the public (Table 10). Yet almost half the corporations undertaking such audits voiced the belief that all corporations will be required to submit to social audits in the future (Table 9).

2. If a social audit is to be made, what activities should be evaluated? What should be the scope of the audit?

A substantial majority of all corporations surveyed assumed responsibility for a variety of social activities, but there is no consensus as to what a social audit should include. Some of the possibilities are:

All social activities being performed, *or* those the corporation deems it advantageous to report on because of special accomplishments or because of special public concern at the moment

Only those activities the corporation is legally obligated to perform, *or* only those undertaken of its own volition

Activities of clear social utility without prospect of profit (e.g., the operation of a day-care center for the children of women workers), *or* activities of equal social utility that are operated for profit (e.g., the operation of schools)[2]

3. Is the making of a social audit feasible? More specifically, can the performance of social activities be measured? Is quantification of performance essential for evaluation?

Survey respondents reported that the inability to measure accomplishments in some or all social activities constituted a principal obstacle to making a social audit. Other respondents, confronted with the problem of quantifying achievements, shied away from use of the term audit. Some suggested the alternative term social report for a statement that would describe but not measure. Still others hold that when you cannot measure what you are speaking about, when you cannot express it in numbers, your knowledge is of a meager and unsatisfactory kind. Can the demand for accountability be met despite the current difficulty of measurement?

Logic of the Social Audit

The steadily increasing demand that corporations account for their performance in a wide variety of social activities was traced in Chapter 1. As was made clear in that description, the corporation, like the government, the hospital, the university, and the church, is being held accountable to its constituencies and to the general public in an unprecedented fashion today.

This demand is an inevitable consequence of the emergence of the compact society in which many more units—business firms, governments, hospitals, colleges, universities, and others—compete with one another in markedly limited living space to serve a people that expect a better quality of life than has previously been available to them. Each unit is being held accountable for contributing to making life safer, more secure, more healthful, more equitable, and more rewarding of honest effort, and to offering greater opportunity for every individual. These two trends (the increasing demand for accountability by the individual unit and the rising expectations as to the acceptable quality of life) underlie the development of the social audit.

These trends have made the determination of what society expects of each unit a critical element of the art of modern-day management. Thomas C. Theobald, executive vice-president of the First National City Bank (New York), articulated this in pragmatic terms: "It's just common sense that if any corporation operates in a social environment, it has to be attuned to it. Otherwise the employees aren't going to like the place, the customers aren't going to be satisfied, and the government is going to be on their back."[3] Despite this recognition, few executives are capable of sensing the expectations of society or are prepared by training or experience to guide their corporations to meet these expectations as well as to fulfill the ever-present demands of the market.

Recognizing these trends, Neil H. Jacoby has advanced a "new theory of enterprise behavior." He calls it " 'the Social Environment Model' because its central tenet is that *the enterprise reacts to the total societal environment and not merely to markets.*"[4] His concept is rooted in the social contract upon which basis the corporation functions. Society in America and elsewhere grants the corporation the right to exist. By issuing a corporate charter, it endows the corporation with certain legal privileges (including a franchise to do business, the privilege of limited liability as an aid to assembling capital, and the right to sue and to be sued as an individual citizen) and many unspecified but valuable rights.

In addition, the corporation enjoys the right, as do all citizens, to the protection of its property (in some measure, overseas as well as at home) by the government. It enjoys the right to retain and to accumulate earnings, thereby avoiding the necessity of going to the market for capital. It can merge with or acquire other companies without having to pay capital gains taxes on appreciated property values. It can compensate its executives in ways that shelter them from taxes that other citizens are obligated to pay. It can acquire market power for products and accumulate economic power sufficient, in some instances, to enable it to influence even the federal government. In return for these and other legal privileges and rights society expects certain standards of behavior.

What society expected in the 1920s in the way of corporate behavior in relation to its customers, its employees, its stockholders, and the general public was markedly different from what is expected in the 1970s.[5] Clearly, even then the corporation was expected to meet certain standards of product quality, to protect its employees against injury, to limit hours of work to no more than 48, to render accurate reports of its finances to its stockholders and to those from whom it sought credit, and to conduct its affairs in ways that did not impose on its neighbors.

In the intervening years society has vastly increased its expectations.[6] For example, the response to greater expectations as to product quality and safety is seen by the labels on today's drugs and foodstuffs giving greater details about use and ingredients and the warning printed on each package of cigarettes. The corporation is now expected to limit hours of work to a five-day week of eight hours a day and to supplement an individual's pay with provision for income in the event he or she is ill, is unemployed, or is retired. The corporation's legal obligation to report on its finances to stockholders and to would-be purchasers of its stock has been further extended and carefully detailed. The general public has come to expect the corporation to eliminate its pollution from the air, the streams, and the environment in general and to accept other customary responsibilities such as contributing to the support of annual community fund-raising drives as well as local colleges and hospitals.

Many of these activities are mandated by law; for example, the provision for employee safety required by the federal Occupational Safety and Health Act of 1970 and the prohibition against environmental pollution. Other activities are effectively prescribed by custom; for example, the provision of support for the universities and hospitals in the areas where major plants or offices are located. Some practices may be impelled by pressure from employees; for example, the provision of day-care centers for children of working mothers and still others reflect the pioneering of progressive employers, such as the establishment of plants in economically disadvantaged areas to provide employment to contribute to the betterment of living conditions.[7]

The establishment of many social programs by corporations reflects the gradual translation of expectations manifested by a portion of the society into obligations enforced at first by public opinion and subsequently enacted into law. For example, well before social security was institutionalized by the federal government, some employers, either voluntarily or at the prodding of unions, provided pensions for their long-time employees. Other corporations pioneered in publicizing the contents of products offered for sale. Some corporations led the way by investing in costly facilities with which to abate pollution. Today, all corporations are obliged by law to engage in these activities.

The corporation has been impelled by society's evolving expectations to assume certain responsibilities. It follows from this that the corporation will be called upon, formally or by the subtle pressures of public opinion, to make known how it is measuring up to its responsibilities. Thus, the social audit flows logically from the social contract and from the expectations rooted in this contract.

Scope of the Social Audit

Historically, the primary *social* responsibility of the corporation has been to discover and develop goods and services that satisfy the needs of people. The accomplishment of that end—the production of an increasing abundance of steadily improving goods and services—has long been regarded as of such great value to the society as to warrant the earning of profits.[8]

As the basic wants for food, clothing, shelter, and health care of most members of American society have been satisfied, society's expectations have grown to include not only new and better goods and services but other things as well. For example: (1) services of clear social utility that were once provided by government and are now provided by corporations at a *profit;* such services include postsecondary education (e.g., the schools and educational services marketed by Bell and Howell Company) and providing food services for school programs and for aged and invalid persons in their homes; (2) a widening range of amenities, services, and information for employees, consumers, shareholders, and the community, without prospect of profit and at the cost of the corporation.

If the social audit is to catalogue all such activities, verify the costs entailed, and evaluate the benefits produced, it becomes an evaluation of everything a corporation is doing. When the scope is thus defined, it becomes impractical to accomplish a social audit and, indeed, the information it would present would likely be too massive to be useful.

If, on the other hand, the scope of the audit—that is, the activities to be catalogued, verified, and evaluated—is limited, it will not demonstrate to the constituencies the extent to which the corporation's social performance measures up to what the constituents expect. For example, the social audit will not perform this principal function if it is limited to (1) those activities for which a corporation's executives are particularly concerned about accomplishments and/or costs incurred; (2) those activities about which information is publicized to better the corporation's public image.

Therefore, the scope of the social audit (like the scope of the financial audit) is determined by the informational needs of those it is designed to serve—employees, consumers, concerned shareholders, the general public, and those who influence the shaping of public opinion. In the course of time those needs will undoubtedly change, but in the main they will include the need for information about: (1) statutorily required activities (e.g., the provision of equal employment opportunities for minority group members); (2) voluntary activities (e.g., the making of contributions to health, educational, and cultural agencies and the "adoption" of a local high school); and (3) socially useful activities undertaken for the making of profits (e.g., contracting to provide teaching services in the schools).

The key task for the corporation is to specify what activities are of concern to its constituencies at a particular time.[9] It is a difficult task, and new ways and means must be developed to accomplish it.

How to Determine the Scope of the Social Audit

Few social audits made today embrace the categories of activities that fall logically within its scope as suggested here. The scope of few if any of these audits is determined by the standard of social expectations that has been proposed. The failure to attain this ideal is to be expected at this early stage in the evolution of this form of appraisal. A methodology for identifying social expectations and appraising corporate social performance is still being developed. To indicate the point that has been reached, we will describe ways of determining what society expects of the corporation and examine existing yardsticks for measuring the corporation's performance of various social activities.

Society communicates its expectations in several ways. This is done through the crusading of reformers. It is also done by businessmen with social foresight who by taking advanced steps communicate the needs of society by example. Such examples have been set by Henry Ford when he established the $5 per-day wage in the automobile industry, by George Eastman and Marion B. Folsom when in the 1930s Eastman Kodak Company established its wage-dividend and pension policies, and by International Business Machines Corporation and Xerox Corporation more recently in granting leaves at full pay to employees who choose to engage in community activities.

Group pressures are another means by which society communicates its expectations. The National Consumers League in the 1930s and the United Farm Workers in 1972 communicated what they contended were the expectations of the society by mobilizing consumers to force employers to better conditions for their workers. Strikes, boycotts, sit-ins, and demonstrations have been used to convey other expectations to corporate leadership.

In theory, society communicates its expectations to corporate leadership through the voices of the corporation's stockholders. Many recent stockholders' meetings illustrate both the theoretical process as well as its ineffectiveness. A score of issues ranging from the corporation's efforts to curb pollution and employ women to changing its operations in South Africa have been presented by small, articulate minorities in the form of resolutions for stockholder approval which have been regularly voted down. The presentation of such resolutions by a few stockholders, despite their usual rejection, nevertheless forces corporate management to consider whether society expects it to perform the actions proposed.

Society conveys its expectations most clearly when they are finally enacted into law. Prior to 1935, a few employers provided pensions for employees who had spent much of their adult life in their employ. Unemployment and suffering among the aged during the depression of the 1930s attracted public concern and resulted in the enactment of the Social Security Act. By means of this law, society converted a growing public desire and the example of a few employers into an obligation for all employers. Other examples of such actions are apparent in the labeling requirements and product quality standards set by the Food and Drug Administration and the Federal Trade Commission, in the water quality standards established by the state governments, and in the financial reporting practices stipulated by the Securities and Exchange Commission.

Such channels of information provided the corporation executive with indications of society's expectations.[10] However, much of what is transmitted through these channels (other than actual legislation) is distorted by the opposing views of others in the society, is blurred by emotions, or is simply inaccurate. The executive is thus left with the task of weighing these messages and deciding what expectations have gained general acceptance among consumers, employers, stockholders, and citizens so strongly as to suggest, if not require, that the corporation take action. His problem is one of determining what social responsibilities are of such critical and continuing importance to the constituencies his firm serves as to warrant its acceptance of the associated costs and obligations.[11]

The methodology to make this determination has not been perfected but is now being developed. Staff members of the larger corporation usually have an understanding of the demands as well as threats made on the company at the present time and those that will be made in the future. What the corporation more often lacks is the capacity for objectively weighing its obligation to meet such demands. Yet some larger companies, General Electric Company, for instance, have made such assessments.[12] They have demonstrated that decisions can be made by staff, when guided by clear policy, about the relationship that the corporation strives to maintain to the society.[13] To ensure objectivity the corporation's staff and managers can be aided by market surveys and polls of constituent opinion that provide reliable indications of social expectations. From the results managers then can select those activities they think they should pursue to meet the most urgent needs of society.

48

The Measurement Problem

Presuming that the scope of a social audit can be determined, what yardsticks are available to measure the costs and accomplishments of activities included in the social audit? Without credible measures of business's social performance the social audit will make little progress. Many business executives hold views similar to that expressed by one respondent to the survey, who stated: "Most of the elements involved cannot be quantified in any meaningful way and ... a balance sheet would result only in an oversimplified representation which might lend itself to puffery." Measures of accomplishment for many activities, as this respondent has accurately pointed out, do not yet exist, and the identification of costs is sometimes difficult. The problems involved in developing measures of accomplishment and in identifying relevant costs are substantial, yet the development of useful measures is progressing.

The financial auditor has numerous acceptable yardsticks for evaluating the financial operations of a business enterprise. They include unit production costs, the ratio of each category of costs to the sales dollar, the current ratio, inventory turnover, the aging of receivables, cash flow analyses, the ratio of net earnings to interest on debt, and others. The social auditor is at an early stage in forging similar yardsticks and faces formidable obstacles in perfecting measures for a number of social activities.

The Bogey of Quantification

The development of the social audit today is hobbled, as our survey indicates, by confusion as to purpose as well as by difficulties confronted in striving to measure costs and accomplishments. If the social audit is to inform insiders alone, one set of measures focusing on costs and efficiency of performance is needed. If the social audit is designed to meet the demands of outsiders for an assessment of social performance, a different set of measures is required.

If we assume that both needs must be served, the problem of measurement still remains. By definition an audit is a "methodical examination and review," but many businessmen view an audit as necessarily involving quantification, and, as we have stated, the quantification of costs and accomplishments is difficult, the latter more so than the former.

The costs involved in many social activities, although not all, are difficult to isolate. The benefits received by the company itself or those contributed to society are difficult to appraise. For example, what cost/benefit is involved in the maintenance by corporations of deposits in minority-owned and -operated banks? In increasing the proportion of blacks in the corporate work force? If the cost of building a plant in the inner city rather than moving it to the suburbs can be identified, how can the auditor measure the benefits produced for the company? For the community? What is the value to society of contributions to the support of black colleges and universities? Of the service of corporate employees on leave to teach in universities? Of the stimulation of interest in liturgical music?

The quantification that is involved in the financial audit (which conditions thinking as to the nature of a social audit) evolved over many years. Gradually accountants have found ways of quantifying concepts that at an earlier time were dealt with only or primarily as subjective judgments (e.g., cash flow). But even today some important concepts of costs and value are difficult to quantify and are treated in descriptive footnotes to corporate financial statements.

Methods for quantifying accomplishments of social activities are being developed. For those activities that·are now required by government, some yardsticks that quantify what is expected have been established; for example, state and federal governments have established air quality and water quality standards. Yardsticks are evolving for some activities that are generally accepted by corporations as responsibilities they should bear, for example, the proportion of net income the corporation contributes to charitable, educational, religious, and welfare institutions. For many activities that corporations have undertaken, no yardsticks of accomplishment are yet available. To illustrate, there are no yardsticks to measure the performance of a company in helping society to improve its transportation systems or to preserve animal life or to recycle materials. A review of the CED list of possible social programs (Table 6) will show that no credible measures exist for the great majority. Gradually ways must and, hopefully, will be found to evaluate the worth as well as the cost of many activities that are now unmeasurable.

To Whom Should the Social Audit Be Made Available?

One-half of the companies responding to our survey stated that they made the results of their audit of social activities available only to the company's executives and directors. Less than half the respondent companies made the results available to stockholders and to the public. Do these practices constitute the kind of accountability being called for?

When one assesses the demands from constituents and the breadth of the social audits being made by the pioneering companies, the answer must be "No." Yet, an increasing number of corporations are now including statements in their annual and quarterly reports to stockholders describing what they have done in particular fields of social activity.[14] A few corporations use newspaper advertising to tell the general public about social activities they are engaged in,* and some others have prepared special reports describing rather comprehensively their activities and have made them generally available.

---

*For example, the Chase Manhattan Bank advertised in a number of newspapers and journals that "We helped the Black magazine (*Black Enterprise*) that's helping Black businessmen."

Examples of such special reports are those made in 1972, 1973, and 1974 by the General Motors Corporation entitled *Report on Progress in Areas of Public Concern*. These reports explain what General Motors did in these years to meet the problems of automobile pollution and automobile safety. They refine and make more generally known the corporation's policy relative to investments in South Africa, its policy and accomplishments in hiring members of minority groups, its efforts to assist minority group members to conduct their own businesses, and its efforts to seek the views of the consumers of its products and act upon their complaints.[†]

Preparing for an Unclear Future

If an assessment of the present practices of corporations regarding the social audit suggests the strong possibility that America's corporations will be expected to assume greater responsibilities and will be held increasingly accountable for the performance of their activities, what then should corporation executives do to equip their firms to meet these obligations? We will strive to answer this question in Chapter 4.

[†]Other companies that distribute similar reports for public consumption include the Bank of America, CNA Financial Corporation, Dayton Hudson Corporation, Eastern Gas and Fuel Associates, and Ford Motor Company.

4
The Future of the Social Audit

Because of the growing pressure for greater corporate accountability, I can foresee the day when [in addition to the annual financial statements] corporations may be required to publish a social audit, certified by independent accountants. (David Rockefeller)[1]

In Chapter 1 the growing pressure for corporate accountability in social activities was depicted. The results of the survey presented in Chapter 2 show how some American corporations are responding to such pressures. In Chapter 3 the logic underlying corporate assumption of social responsibilities was discussed and the feasibility of auditing the performance of such activities was examined. In the light of these analyses, what may one foresee that corporation executives will do in the years ahead to ensure that their firms meet evolving social obligations?

Since, as we have indicated, a consensus about the nature and purpose of the business social audit is absent today and cannot be expected in the near future, one can easily forecast that the social audit will take many forms, be the subject of much experimentation, and evolve slowly into maturity. One thing, however, seems clear: The social audit will evolve as a means of meeting society's demand for a fuller accountability. In time, although not necessarily soon, a consensus as to its content and form acceptable to both corporations and their constituents will develop. In this final chapter we reach toward the future by presenting a social auditing/

reporting model to provoke discussion and guide corporate practice.

Clarifying Policy Stance

In 1968 Emilio G. Collado summarized the conclusions of business leaders participating in a CED symposium in these words: "The corporation as such should identify those social problems on which its particular resources and skills can be most effectively brought to bear, and make these virtually as much a part of its business objectives as traditional commercial activities."[2] The identification of such problems and the application of corporate resources have made progress in the intervening years. As pointed out earlier, steps in these directions have been impelled by external pressures and by a growing awareness among corporation executives that many or most business decisions have an impact on the society, and that many social problems are of such importance to business that the corporation must determine what it can and should do about them. This awareness has prompted a few corporations to formulate social policies and to integrate social considerations with their business planning. However, the formulation by most corporations of a clear-cut policy as to what responsibilities they will accept has still not taken place.

One admirable model of a corporate social policy statement is that which has been developed by Exxon Corporation.[3] A prototype of business planning that takes into account social considerations is provided by the planning practices of the General Electric Company.[4] An additional illustration is a set of social policies prepared by one of the authors.[5] Few corporations have as yet followed these examples.

Most corporations that have acted have responded to pressures without reasoning why,[6] but now they are asking themselves: Why should we be performing these activities? The next logical step would be the formulation of corporate social policies, but before that step is taken it should be preceded by what Nicholas B. Katzenbach (vice-president and general counsel, International Business Machines Corporation and former U.S. attorney general) has described as a "greening of the boardroom." If the corporation has come to recognize a broadening array of responsibilities to the community and consumers as well as to employees and stockholders, it is logical that boards of directors should include members capable of representing the interests of society as a whole. Such directors provide views that supplement and offer a countervailing voice to the executive management. Within recent years, as a consequence, several score of corporations have elected individuals whose role has been to serve as "public" directors.[7] The choices made in numerous instances, however, raise questions as to whether the individuals selected represent particular segments of the society (particularly blacks and women) or the public interest generally.

Interaction: Policy and Execution

Corporate social policy, although finally formalized by the board of directors, is in fact developed daily by executives in the succession of decisions that they make. And unfortunately, as Arthur B. Toan, Jr., chairman of the AICPA's Committee on Social Measurement, has contended, "in relatively few instances" have firms that are engaged in social activities "developed or (are) developing a modus operandi for decision making, planning, and operational control which . . . take both economic and social considerations into balanced account."[8]

The substance from which corporate social policy is eventually distilled arises from a number of executives' decisions; for example, decisions having to do with the transfer or dismissal of employees of a plant being closed; decisions concerning how long and how thoroughly new products will be tested before release to consumers and how these products shall be advertised and labeled; decisions about whether costly investments to eliminate air or water pollution shall be made or deferred; and decisions relating to whether corporate resources shall be contributed to help eliminate slum housing, to support local colleges, or to build community hospitals. Executives must make or recommend decisions on these and other issues of a social nature. The major decisions, in terms of resources involved or the innovative aspect of the action to be taken, may be ratified by the board of directors, but corporation executives must face these issues first, and for that task they need a policy that is agreed upon and one to which the corporation is committed.[9]

Approaches to the Social Audit

At any one time the expectations of society that are communicated to the corporation (see Chapter 3, "The Logic, Scope, and Feasibility of the Corporate Social Audit") are likely to exceed the corporation's ability to respond to them.[10] In determining which expectations of society he will meet, the executive draws on such policy as has been hammered out and on his own commitment. Gradually organizations are being built and techniques are being developed to meet this task— that is, to determine society's expectations at the moment and to determine which expectations the executive can (and should) make a part of the corporation's operating plans.

Organizational Arrangements

The nature of a corporation's (and its executives') commitment to the meeting of society's expectations is often reflected by the person or group within the company to whom it assigns responsibility for "reading" society's expectations and for recommending what activities the company shall undertake; for persistent monitoring of the performance of each division and each subsidiary company; for seeing to it that the results of an assessment of performance are regularly made available to corporate executives and directors; and for recommending what results shall be made available to stockholders and the public and how they shall be made available.

Assignment of all or most of these responsibilities to a public relations department suggests that the corporation believes that social responsibilities are undertaken to improve the corporate image. Assignment of such responsibilities to a personnel department suggests a limit on the range of activities that will be undertaken and a concentration on the concerns of employees. Creation of an organizational unit (such as the urban affairs division of the American Telephone & Telegraph Company) or a senior executive position (such as the position of executive vice-president for social policy at the Bank of America) to be responsible for each of the activities enumerated above suggests a responsiveness to the changing role of the corporation in American society. One can reasonably forecast the establishment of such organizational arrangements in an increasing proportion of major corporations.

Assessing Society's Expectations

As yet there are few indications as to how corporate executives, other than by seat-of-the-pants judgments, can determine which expectations deserve priority among those being communicated to him by reformers, consumer advocates, some shareholders, the practices of other corporations, and government (see Chapter 3, p. 42). Much of what is communicated through these channels (other than the actual enactment of legislation) is distorted by the contradictory views of others in the society, is blurred by emotions, or is infeasible. The corporate executive, hence, is left with the necessity of weighing the messages conveyed via the channels other than legislation and deciding what expectations have gained such general acceptance among consumers, employees, stockholders, and citizens as strongly to suggest, if not require, his taking action. The corporate executive's problem is one of determining what social problems are of such critical and continuing consequence to the constituencies his firm serves as to warrant the company's acceptance of some measure of responsibility for aiding and for shouldering the associated costs and obligations.

A Case Study

Consider, for example, an executive of an electric utility company serving the eastern third of a major industrial state. His company's service area encompasses three principal metropolitan areas. Its consumers, employees, suppliers, bankers, and a considerable proportion of its noninstitutional stockholders are concentrated in these areas. Identifiable voices propose that his company make major investments to curb pollution, that it hire more blacks and more women, that it name women and blacks to its board, and that it provide greater support for two local colleges and for still other purposes. How does the executive weigh the desirability and critical nature of these responsibilities thrust upon his company, in addition to responsibilities already being borne (e.g., participation in the federal JOBS program, support of the Boy Scouts, lending executives to assist in curriculum planning in local high schools, and making capital gifts to hospitals in two of the major cities)? In somewhat simplified terms, the task has three elements.

The first part of the task is to identify the constituencies in each metropolitan area whose views need be known and to establish methods for sampling their opinions. The constituencies will likely include, in addition to those associated with the company on an economic basis, local organizations and officials whose views may be expected to reflect the opinions of influential groups within the community.

The second element of the task is to frame the demands being made upon the corporation in such a way that a reliable sample of constituents may indicate the priority they attach to each. For example, in the opinion of constituents is it more important for the company to invest $1 million in equipment to curb pollution or to contribute $1 million to the building fund of a local college? Should the company employ new workers to reduce local unemployment if this will increase operating costs by x percent and involve an increase of electric rates by y percent? This approach to the measurement of priorities requires the careful and objective statement of each alternative and involves costly private interviews. However, without the results of such inquiries, the executive and his board will lack the kind of information that they can rely upon.

The third part of the task is to poll constituents and analyze the results to obtain a reliable reading of the expectations of the community being served. This task requires techniques and skills that are well developed in opinion and consumer research but are not commonly found in the employ of an electric utility. They require an order of objectivity and impartiality so great as to argue strongly that this task be assigned to an agency independent of the corporation itself.

The results of such an assessment of the expectations of consumers, employees, stockholders, and citizens will not eliminate the need for executive judgment, but they will provide information to guide decision making about what social responsibilities, in addition to those specified by government, the company may strive to meet.

As sophisticated an approach as this to the assessment of constituent expectations will not likely be generally adopted soon. Prevailing practices suggest that during the 1970s most corporate decision making about what social responsibilities shall be assumed will be based on hunch, example, and of course government edict. Undoubtedly, however, examples set by other "lead" corporations will be influential in gradually shaping general practice.

Evolution of a Social Report

Most of the social audits reported on in Chapter 2 were not undertaken in response to the demand for accountability. However, as trends of recent years indicate, pressure is growing for both social performance and accountability for that performance, and executive "feel for the situation" will no longer be the only criterion for determining a corporation's involvement. In fact, it would be appropriate to assume that in the future all corporations will be required to submit a social audit to the public. (Forty-six percent of the respondents to the survey made this assumption.)

If this forecast is valid, how are corporations likely to meet this demand for accountability? An accounting maxim specifies that "the uses to which information will be put should govern both the conceptual and procedural bases on which information is prepared and disseminated."[11] This suggests that to satisfy the demand for accountability, corporations will continue, by trial and error, to develop ways of assessing and reporting on social performance in forms that will provide constituents with information as to how the corporation is responding to society's expectations and how it compares with other corporations in the same geographical area and/or the same industry.

To make information available that would permit an informed evaluation of a corporation's response to society's expectations by those who demand accountability, we suggest the social auditing/reporting model illustrated in Exhibit 1. This model does not provide a response to every demand that is voiced nor does it provide a single measure of a corporation's aggregate social performance. Rather, it presents a comprehensive report of what the corporation is doing and has done, and places the burden of evaluation on readers of the report.

The model presumes that the corporation, by such methods as it chooses, has identified society's expectations, has determined the priority each deserves, and has accepted responsibility for some or many. Once the corporation has taken these steps, the model proposes that it report which expectations it recognizes, which expectations it can and is responding to, and the results of an assessment of its performance in each activity it is conducting. This effort would involve the steps given in Exhibit 1.

Exhibit 1

A Model for Social Auditing/Reporting

1. An Enumeration of Social Expectations and the Corporation's Response	A summary and candid enumeration by program areas (e.g., consumer affairs, employee relations, physical environment, local community development) of what is expected, and the corporation's reasoning as to why it has undertaken certain activities and not undertaken others.
2. A Statement of the Corporation's Social Objectives and the Priorities Attached to Specific Activities	For each program area the corporation would report what it will strive to accomplish and what priority it places on the activities it will undertake.
3. A Description of the Corporation's Goals in Each Program Area and of the Activities It Will Conduct	For each priority activity, the corporation will state a specific goal (in quantitative terms when possible) and describe how it is striving to reach that goal (e.g., to better educational facilities in the community it will make available qualified teachers from among members of its staff).
4. A Statement Indicating the Resources Committed to Achieve Objectives and Goals	A summary report, in quantitative terms, by program area and activity, of the costs—direct and indirect—assumed by the corporation.
5. A Statement of the Accomplishments and/or Progress Made in Achieving Each Objective and Each Goal	A summary, describing in quantitative measures when feasible and through objective, narrative statement when quantification is impracticable, the extent of achievement of each objective and each goal.

Making Credible a Social Report

If the model for auditing and reporting outlined above is used, the nature of the corporation's social commitment could be effectively judged by the corporation's choice of the social expectations it will respond to, its definition of objectives and goals, the activities it undertakes, the resources it commits, and the accomplishments it reports. The report should provide sufficiently detailed information to enable readers—executives within the corporation or members of the public outside it—to compare the corporation's social program with those of other corporations operating in the same locality or the same industry. As yardsticks for the measurement of accomplishment gradually gain acceptance, or are mandated by government, they can be utilized to add specificity to the report and to facilitate comparison.

In the absence of consensus about what social responsibilities the corporation is obligated to discharge and about the standards of performance that should prevail with respect to each social activity undertaken (e.g., what proportion of its net income should a corporation contribute to the support of educational and health institutions), the credibility of a corporate social audit rests on the comprehensiveness and candor with which results are reported. Two courses of action will lend assurance that such comprehensiveness and candor will be achieved.

The first step is the retention of an independent analyst to examine the corporation's performance and to prepare and certify the report. Qualified independent analysts are scarce, but a few of the national management consulting firms, a few of the national accounting firms, and a few members of the faculties of graduate schools of business possess the requisite competence.

The second step is to have a committee composed of members of the board of directors (including public directors) review and approve the social report. A few companies have established board committees to consider issues of social responsibility.* These committees, often called the public affairs committee, the urban affairs committee, or the social policy committee, are, in each company cited above, composed of some (or all) public directors. Moreover, these

---

*Such committees have been established, for example, by ARA Services, Celanese Corporation, Ford Motor Company, General Motors Corporation, International Business Machines Corporation, Kimberly-Clark Corporation, and Philip Morris.

committees logically include those directors that bring to their deliberations a broad understanding of the society and its needs. For example, Vernon E. Jordan, executive director of the National Urban League, serves on the Celanese committee; James R. Killian, former president of the Massachusetts Institute of Technology, serves on the General Motors committee; and J. George Harrar, former president of the Rockefeller Foundation, serves on the analogous committee of Kimberly-Clark's board of directors. The committee's review and approval of the independent report would be essentially analogous to the action of the corporate audit committee, which in many corporations meets with the independent accountants, reviews a draft of their financial report, and approves this report before it is promulgated to the stockholders and to the public.

The CED statement on the *Social Responsibilities of Business Corporations* issued in June 1971 declared: "Business functions by public consent, and its basic purpose is to serve constructively the needs of society—to the satisfaction of society."[12] The demands for information voiced by reformers, consumers, investors, government, and the public in general constitute a continuing and expanding effort to appraise how well business is serving the needs of society. The corporate social audit is, for those companies that have pioneered in the making of such assessments of their own social performance, a tool by which they can demonstrate how constructively and how comprehensively they are serving the needs of the society. We hope this book will picture for businessmen the state of the art of social auditing and suggest the directions in which they may be expected to proceed during the years ahead.

Appendix

Question 9:

In general, do you think that business firms will be required to make a social audit in the future? If your answer is yes, please indicate whether in your opinion this prospect is acceptable to you as a businessman.

In the near future—No; longer range—perhaps Yes. Audit itself will not eliminate need to be responsive to society around the business corporation.

Yes, it places a healthy discipline on management to perform.

If company has major impact on social problem—e.g., environment, employment—it should feel obligated to account for itself.

Not as a matter of *Law*, this is required in certain specific activities, i.e., equal employment records. Reporting on a total basis is not likely.

A legal requirement is perhaps unlikely near term. However, other pressures—both internal and external—are likely to result in more social analysis and publication by business.

Yes: It's a matter of being responsive to a changing climate of public attitudes and demands, the costs for which will inevitably be reflected in the price for the company's service.

Audit may be a misleading term. We have opted for a representative inventory instead. Could an acceptable methodology for the social audit be devised, we would welcome it.

Acceptable—already required in such areas as affirmative action.

Possibly in the long term, but not short range.

I would hope not; it's not clear that the social audit would be necessary or useful to all businesses. A "requirement" that all businesses undertake the audit might vitiate the purpose.

It is acceptable and necessary but danger lies in making comparisons and in measuring results.

Answer assumes audit will most likely be descriptive rather than quantitative, and that the future is yet some way off—allowing time to become "acceptable."

No way of predicting, but current government regulations make this mandatory in many areas.

This is a qualified "yes"—the "requirement" may not be greater than the type of EEO, OSHA, and EPA reporting now mandated.

The prospect is not only acceptable but I deem it to be necessary. We do not operate in a vacuum. Lou Golden's book *Only by Public Consent* points out the urgency of the situation and should be required reading.

If you mean legally required by government action, then—No; if by the consumer marketplace, then perhaps—Yes.

The answer is "No" if required legally within the next ten years; after that "Yes." It would be a good idea if for no other reason than to show the costs of socially related activities that ultimately are borne by the customer.

Acceptability would be a factor of content and scope of audit. If confined to those matters which a corporation can reasonably influence and cope with in its assigned function within society an audit would be acceptable.

If reasonably done—i.e., not in response to group pressures.

Not in the near future. I think companies will want to do it for their own purposes.

Believe it will become acceptable.

I personally feel this must be voluntary in order to be effective. If it should be required, it is not acceptable to me. The requirement may evolve from necessity and enlightened self-interest.

Acceptable and desirable.

No, because of impossibility of putting numbers on concepts.

Yes, since we will be responding to public demand.

But not for a long time since we lack clear techniques. Personally, the sooner the better.

Business firms should conduct internal social audits.

Over the *long run* possibly "Yes"—at least in areas now showing up in shareholder proxy proposals—South Africa, pollution control, broader representation of social concerns at the board level, etc.

Yes, provided that acceptable and creditable methods and measures of performance can be developed.

The definite trend toward "people" considerations, and less emphasis on materialism, will require more regular and objective social audits in the future.

Seems inevitable and will probably be mandatory by legislation if not done on a voluntary basis by business. Major concern is getting public to believe what business reports.

(required underlined) Acceptable.
Yes, but in specific areas, e.g., equal employment, pollution, etc.

We have always believed that social responsibility is a primary ingredient of every sound business enterprise.

Question is ridiculous!

The type of audit, together with how the results are to be used, will determine whether it will be acceptable.

Social and public pressure will require it. Internal audit by the company itself rather than an external agency would be acceptable.

It will help the banking industry make a correct appraisal of the needs, the priorities, and the remedies. Companies should take the initiative before they are required to do so.

COMMENT: Prospects of legislation mandating formal social audits are remote since sanctions to achieve social responsibility can be imposed by specific legislation or regulations.

I thing they *should* move toward it.

Acceptable so long as there is————understanding that as business accepts more and more of the social burden it is less and less effective competitively with the (global?) economy.

Yes, if done well and generally supported and realistic standards are available.

Yes, but not on specific terms. Probably a listing and dollars—but community needs differ so there can be no standardization.

If it is reasonable and not subject to pressures on company that will have a material effect on efficiency.

We do not actively promote the idea at this time but would certainly be willing to make a social audit available to the public as long as we can be the ones to determine the contents of the audit and the manner in which it's presented.

It is acceptable if reasonable social audit standards are established and enough lead time is given to corporations to perform a social audit.

Yes, if acceptable measures of performance can be developed; otherwise, reports or specific activities will suffice.

Fully acceptable as long as one industry or one company is not subjected to disproportionate pressure.

Social audit could be beneficial if reasonable standards are evolved as to what should be concluded and how performance is measured.

While acceptable, in my opinion little is gained by too narrow audits done on basis of activities measured only in dollars, especially for large organizations in the service rather than manufacturing sector.

Yes—within reasonable guidelines and definitions.

Yes, but will entail significant costs to business which should be publicly disclosed.

Not a quantified audit—but certainly increased appraisals on issues of importance.

It is acceptable. As the basic idea or understanding of business-social relationships permeates management (hopefully through inclusion of this aspect of management in curriculum in our universities as well as government action, minority group pressure, etc.), companies will report more naturally and more fully on their "social" involvements. Now we must push for such reporting. Later, it will be expected, routine.

OSHA, EPA, EEOC, FTC, etc., can require reviews in their areas of performance.

Business is being asked to adopt a more sensitive and responsive attitude toward the overall social problems of our country. This is something business should do, and it will be required to account more fully for its involvement as time goes on.

If "required" in sense of necessary for company's own self-assessment, this is acceptable. Audits of this nature should not be required by regulation or law.

We do not believe that this will present any serious problems.

Yes, as long as some adequate measures for comparing various companies' performances are developed.

It is accepted and welcomed—social audits will be provided by business voluntarily for a number of different reasons.

To a great extent the active participation of any company in the affairs of the community ultimately result in positive contributions to the profit of the company. In this context, social audits, if not carried to wild extremes, are not only acceptable but necessary.

Required social audits are, I think, inevitable. Under those circumstances business has no choice. At least the information would be more accurate and complete and, therefore, more acceptable.

Pressure will continue from certain groups—but a requirement by regulatory edict is far off in our opinion.

Since we expect to be required to do this as a part of the rate-making process, we may as well derive any benefits we can from it.

To inventory and assess a company's social action programs is good business and should be followed by all companies.

Not with present state-of-the-art.

I am not optimistic as to the guidelines that may be established for social audits.

We think that it is good business practice for corporations continually to evaluate and reassess their position and performance in the social and physical environment. Whether it will be "required" and if so, by whom, is not certain in our opinion.

Yes.

The acceptability will be governed by the manner in which such information is published.

It is acceptable, but the requirement to audit will be fragmented, not comprehensive as your definition suggests.

It will be acceptable if a reasonable method of accounting can be developed to reflect efforts made in this area.

Such things as hiring quotas appear to be in the cards. This will have an adverse impact on operating efficiency.

Public statements of social involvement are good public relations—directly or indirectly affecting the decisions of prospective and current customers, investors, and employees.

It is acceptable in some areas, such as equal employment opportunity. It must recognize that, particularly in the case of regulated public utilities, the company has obligations to its security holders, employees, stockholders, and to the customers whom it serves. In general business will find it necessary to make a greater public accounting of their social responsibility activities. However, the feasibility of measuring these activities in quantitative financial terms is questionable and, therefore, the social audit as a corollary to financial reports is unlikely.

It would depend on who made the requirement. If it were made by our stockholders, it would be acceptable to our company.

Within limits.

Unlikely as a *requirement*. However, may become a voluntary standard practice.

Is reasonable and acceptable but must be done in context of providing adequate profits to attract capital.

Certainly not until a meaningful measurement is developed.

The public will want to know what business is doing to discharge its social responsibilities. Forward-thinking businesses will make sure their efforts and successes are visible.

Contributors

John J. Corson is a director of ARA Services, Inc., and the American Sterilizer Company and serves as a trustee of six educational institutions. Formerly he served as a management consultant with McKinsey & Co., Inc. (1951–1966) and with Fry Consultants, Inc. (1969–1973), and as a professor, Princeton University (1962–1966). He is the author of many books; the most recent is a reissue of the 1960 publication *The Governance of Colleges and Universities.*

Robert C. Meehan is a management consultant with Peat, Marwick, & Mitchell & Co. He was formerly deputy treasurer and comptroller with the Committee for Economic Development. He received an M.B.A. from Columbia University in 1971 and a B.A. from the New School for Social Research in 1969.

Alfred C. Neal is president of the Committee for Economic Development. Before coming to CED in 1956 he was first vice-president and director of research of the Federal Reserve Bank of Boston. His government service has included membership on the (Williams) Commission on International Trade and Investment Policy, the Commission on Foreign Economic Policy (Randall Commission), and several other government advisory boards.

George A. Steiner is professor of management and public policy in the Graduate School of Management, University of California at Los Angeles. He is also director of the Center for Research and Dialogue on Business in Society. He has been director of policy development in both the Defense Production Administration and the Office of Defense Mobilization during the Korean War and has served as a consultant to many government agencies and business corporations. His best-known books include *Issues in Business and Society* (1974) and *Top Management Planning,* 2d ed. (1974).

Notes

Chapter 1

1. *Du Pont Cavalcade of Television Plans Exciting 1973–74 Season,* a leaf-let distributed to stockholders by the Stockholder Relations Division of the E. I. du Pont de Nemours and Company with the quarterly dividend payment in September 1973.
2. Committee for Economic Development, *Social Responsibilities of Business Corporations,* A Statement on National Policy by the Research and Policy Committee of the Committee for Economic Development (New York, June 1971), p. 15.
3. Ibid., p. 16.
4. *New York Times,* 24 January 1971, sec. 3, pp. 1, 9.
5. Ibid. Theodore J. Jacobs makes the further point that "neither the regulator's zeal nor the business executive's conscience is a substitute for continual monitoring and participation by those affected by corporate power, the voluntary and involuntary consumers." "Pollution, Consumerism, Accountability," *Center Magazine* 5, no. 1 (January-February 1972): 46.
6. Robert A. Dahl, "A Prelude to Corporate Reform," *Business and Society Review,* no. 1 (Spring 1972), pp. 17–23.
7. Ibid., pp. 21–23.
8. Neil H. Jacoby, "The Business Corporation in Social Service: Its Role as Problem Solver for Government" (Paper presented to the Conference on the Corporation and the Quality of Life, Center for the Study of Democratic Institutions, Santa Barbara, Calif., September 27–October 1, 1971).
9. For example, see Vance O. Packard, *The Waste Makers* (New York: David McKay Co., 1960).
10. For a discussion, in well-reasoned detail, of the need and the growing insistence of consumers for timely, intelligible, relevant, truthful, and complete information, see John A. Howard and James Hulbert, "Advertising and the Public Interest" (Staff report prepared for the Federal Trade Commission, April 1973). This recommends actions by the Federal Trade Commission, the Food and Drug Administration, the Federal Communications Commission, the Executive Office of the President, Congress, the courts, and consumer interest groups that would ensure the availability of such information.
11. For development of this reasoning, see William H. Donaldson (Address delivered at the Annual Convention of the National Council on Teacher Retirement, Louisville, Ky., October 7, 1971). Donaldson is chairman and chief executive officer of Donaldson, Lufkin and Jenrette.
12. For a statement on investment philosophy, see Russell Sage Foundation, *Annual Report 70–71* (New York, 1972), p. 71.
13. For an analysis and recommendations concerning the role the university should play as an investor, see John G. Simon, Charles W. Powers, and

Jon P. Gunnemann, *The Ethical Investor: Universities and Corporate Responsibility* (New Haven: Yale University Press, 1972).

14. "Principles for the Guidance of Bank Fiduciaries in Dealing with Issues of Corporate Social Responsibility," in American Bankers Association, Trust Division, *Trust Principles and Policies* (Washington, D.C., 1973).

15. Council on Economic Priorities, *Paper Profits: Pollution in the Pulp and Paper Industry* (New York, 1972).

16. U.S. Securities and Exchange Commission, SEC Release No. 33-5343 (Washington, D.C., December 1972); and a revised Release No. 33-5427, which contained proposed amendments to Rule 3-08 of Regulation 5-X.

17. SEC Release No. 33-5120 (July 1971).

18. Murray L. Weidenbaum, "Social Responsibility Is Closer Than You Think," *Michigan Business Review* 25, no. 4 (July 1973): 32–40.

19. *Wall Street Journal*, 30 October 1973, p. 18. See also the decision in Stephen Fischer et al. *v.* Michael Kletz et al., 249 F. Supp. 539 (1966), in which the U.S. District Court, S.D. New York, stated that "the public accountant must report fairly on the facts as he finds them whether favorable or unfavorable to his client. His duty is to safeguard the public interest, not that of his client."

20. For an enumeration and description of ten principles of socioeconomic accounting, see David F. Linowes, "The Accounting Profession and Social Progress," *Journal of Accountancy* 136, no. 1 (July 1973): 32–40.

21. David F. Linowes, "Socio-Economic Accounting," *Journal of Accountancy* 126, no. 5 (November 1968): 37–42.

23. Arthur B. Toan, "Social Information and Social Measurement" (Paper presented to the Committee on Social Measurement, American Institute of Certified Public Accountants, Denver, Colo., September 7, 1972).

24. Steven C. Dilley and Jerry J. Weygandt, "Measuring Social Responsibility: An Empirical Test," *Journal of Accountancy* 136, no. 3 (September 1973): 62–70.

25. David F. Linowes, "Let's Get on with the Social Audit: A Specific Proposal," *Business and Society Review/Innovation*, no. 4 (Winter 1972–73), pp. 39–42.

26. Committee for Economic Development, *Social Responsibilities of Business Corporations*, p. 16.

27. Ibid., p. 46.

28. *New York Times Magazine*, 13 September 1970, p. 126.

29. John J. Corson, *Business in the Humane Society* (New York: McGraw-Hill Book Company, 1971); George A. Steiner, "Social Policies for Business," *California Management Review* 15, no. 2 (Winter 1972): 17–24; and George A. Steiner, *Business and Society*, 2d ed. (New York: Random House, 1974).

30. "What Should a Corporation Do?" *Roper Report*, no. 2 (October 1971), p. 2.

31. U.S. Chamber of Commerce, *Business and the Consumer—A Program for the Seventies* (Washington, D.C., 1970), p. 3.

32. Daniel Bell, *The Coming of Post-Industrial Society: A Venture in Social Forecasting* (New York: Basic Books, 1973), pp. 269–298.

33. A very recent volume (Robin Marris, ed., *The Corporate Society*, New York: Halsted Press, 1974), which presents the views of ten economists and sociologists prominent in this country and Great Britain, stresses two characteristics of the American society in the seventies: (1) In today's highly urbanized, technological society publicly supplied goods (e.g., education, police protection, urban transportation, consumer protection, and protection of the environment) are of large and growing importance; (2) there has been "an extraordinary growth of problems [as the public goods cited illustrate] that are *not* spontaneously solved by market mechanisms" (pp. 302–303).

34. For a description of three methods for approximating the value of a firm's human organization and various forms of goodwill, see Rensis Likert, "The Influence of Social Research on Corporate Responsibility," in William J. Baumol et al. *A New Rationale for Corporate Social Policy* (New York: Committee for Economic Development, 1970), pp. 20–38. For an approximation by a consulting firm of social benefits and costs to four categories (to the staff, to the community, to the general public, and to the firm's clients), see Abt Associates, "Social Income Statement" (Cambridge, Mass.: December 31, 1971).

35. For a description of this approach, see Bernard L. Butcher, "The Program Management Approach to the Corporate Social Audit," in *The Unstable Ground: Corporate Social Policy in a Dynamic Society*, ed. S. Prakash Sethi (Los Angeles: Melville Publishing Company, 1974), pp. 98–106.

36. Clark Abt, "Social Audits—The State of the Art" (Presented at Conference on Corporate Social Responsibility, New York, October 1972).

37. David F. Linowes, "Measuring Social Programs in Business," *Social Audit Seminar—Selected Proceedings* (Washington, D.C.: Public Affairs Council, July 1972).

Chapter 2

1. Eli Goldston, *The Quantification of Concern: Some Aspects of Social Accounting* (Pittsburgh: Carnegie-Mellon University, 1971), p. 15.

2. For example, see Howard R. Bowen, *Social Responsibilities of the Businessman* (New York: Harper and Brothers, 1953), pp. 155–156.

3. Thomas J. Watson, Jr., "is said to have observed that no one expects much in the way of business statesmanship from a company making a few millions, but from one making hundreds of millions a great deal is expected." Edward S. Mason, "The Corporation in the Post-Industrial State," *California Management Review* 12, no. 4 (Summer 1970): 11.

Chapter 3

1. Neil H. Jacoby, *Corporate Power and Social Responsibility: A Blueprint for the Future* (New York: Macmillan Company, 1973), p. 61.

2. George P. Doherty, "Case Study: The Bell and Howell Schools," in *The Future in the Making: Current Issues in Higher Education, 1973,* ed. Dyckman W. Vermilye (San Francisco: Jossey-Bass, 1973).

3. *Washington Evening Star,* 7 March 1972.

4. Jacoby, *Corporate Power and Social Responsibility,* p. 194.

5. Henry Ford II has said: "As customers, as employees, and as citizens, people are expecting many more things, and very different things, from business than they ever have expected in the past." "The Contrast between Industry and Society," *Harvard Business School Bulletin* 46, no. 3 (May-June 1970): 13. For additional recognition of the rising expectations of society, see Joseph F. Cullman III, "The Corporate Social Mandate" (Baccalaureate address delivered at Bellarmine College, Louisville, Ky., May 13, 1973).

6. Melvin Anshen, "Changing the Social Contract: A Role for Business," *Columbia Journal of World Business* 5, no. 6 (November-December 1970): 6–14.

7. For a comprehensive compilation of activities emanating from these several sources, see U.S. Senate, Committee on Commerce, *Initiatives in Corporate Responsibility* (Washington, D.C.: U.S. Government Printing Office, 1972).

8. Criticisms of the "large corporation as a malevolent conscious force" ignore the central fact that "the large bureaucratized industrial enterprise is the principal tool that we have available for providing those resources which are needed to improve the quality of life." Joseph L. Bower, "On the Amoral Organization," in Marris, *The Corporate Society,* p. 178.

9. For a list of fourteen major constituencies likely to exert pressure that the corporation must consider in its strategic planning processes, see Ian H. Wilson, "Reforming the Strategic Planning Process: Integration of Social Responsibility and Business Needs," in Sethi, *The Unstable Ground,* pp. 245–255.

10. For views that have aided us in developing this analysis, see Dow Votaw, "Corporate Social Reform: An Educator's Viewpoint"; and George P. Hinckley and James E. Post, "The Performance Context of Corporate Responsibility," in Sethi, *The Unstable Ground,* pp. 14–23; 293–302.

11. For an ingenious method for making such determinations, see Allan D. Shocker and S. Prakash Sethi, "An Approach to Incorporating Social Preferences in Developing Corporate Action Strategies," in Sethi, *The Unstable Ground,* pp. 67–80.

12. For a discussion and evaluation of some ninety-seven demands made in this company, see Robert M. Estes, "Today's Demands on Business," in *The Changing Business Role in Modern Society,* ed. George A. Steiner (Los Angeles: University of California at Los Angeles, Graduate School of Management, 1974), pp. 160–178.

13. For an excellent example of such policy, see "What Should a Corporation Do?" *Roper Report,* no. 2 (October 1971), pp. 2–3. This contains an

excerpt of the philosophy and goals of the Standard Oil Company (N.J.), now the Exxon Corporation.

14. Fry Consultants, *Social Responsibilities II* (Washington, D.C., 1971), p. 2.

Chapter 4

1. *New York Times,* 1 May 1972, p. 33.
2. Emilio G. Collado, "Toward a More Productive Dialogue" *Saturday Review,* 13 January 1968, p. 62.
3. "What Should a Corporation Do?" *Roper Report,* no. 2 (October 1971), pp. 2–3.
4. Wilson, "Reforming the Strategic Planning Process."
5. Steiner, "Social Policies for Business."
6. For example, Frank Koch wrote that "corporations pride themselves on rational decision making. But when it comes to something as important as their philanthropic efforts, almost everything is left to chance." "Philanthropy: Still the Corporate Stepchild," *Business and Society Review/Innovation,* no. 5 (Spring 1973), p. 88.
7. Bell, *The Coming of Post-Industrial Society,* p. 296; and Phillip I. Blumberg, "Reflections on Proposals for Corporate Reform Through Change in the Composition of the Board of Directors: 'Special Interest' or 'Public' Directors," in Sethi, *The Unstable Ground,* pp. 112–134.
8. Toan, "Social Information and Social Measurement."
9. For an effective statement of this thesis, see William H. Donaldson (Address delivered at the Annual Convention of the National Council on Teacher Retirement, Louisville, Ky., October 7, 1971).
10. Neil W. Chamberlain, in his *The Limits of Corporate Responsibility* (New York: Basic Books, 1973), contends that corporate executives need not fear that expectations will be unduly burdensome. So many individuals in the American society (employees, stockholders, suppliers, and customers) have such substantial stakes in corporations, and such a large proportion of Americans share the values typified by the corporate system, e.g., material abundance, autonomy, equal opportunity, and competitive achievement (pp. 10, 205), that only incremental change will be imposed. This point of view is challenged, however, by the widespread and growing importance of public goods and the apparent concern with the "externalities" that corporate actions impose on society.
11. Dwight R. Ladd, *Contemporary Corporate Accounting and the Public* (Homewood, Ill.: Richard D. Irwin, 1963), p. 17.
12. Committee for Economic Development, *Social Responsibilities of Business Corporations,* p. 11.

DATE DUE

DISPLAY			
Emphasis '82			
JUL 19 83			
JUL 6 1983			
OCT 11 1983			
SEP 22 1983			
GAYLORD			PRINTED IN U.S.A.